The Effortless Pen

Unlocking Creativity with Automatic Writing Tools

Copyright © 2023 by RK Books

All rights reserved.

No part of this publication may be reproduced, distributed, or transmitted in any form or by any means, including photocopying, recording, or other electronic or mechanical methods, without the prior written permission of the publisher, except in the case of brief quotations embodied in critical reviews and certain other noncommercial uses permitted by copyright law.

This book is a work of fiction. Names, characters, places, and incidents are products of the author's imagination or are used fictitiously. Any resemblance to actual events, locales, or persons, living or dead, is entirely coincidental.

Published by |

Table of Contents

Introduction 1

Chapter 1 Understanding Automatic Writing 4

    What Is Automatic Writing? 4

    Historical Perspective of Automatic Writing 8

    Benefits of Automatic Writing 11

    Common Misconceptions About Automatic Writing: Separating Fact from Fiction. 16

Chapter 2 Preparing for Automatic Writing 21

    Creating a Writing Space for Automatic Writing: Cultivating the Ideal Environment 21

    Tools and Materials for Automatic Writing: Equipping Yourself for Creative Exploration 26

    Setting Intentions for Your Automatic Writing Practice: Guiding Your Inner Journey 30

    Clearing Your Mind. 35

Chapter 3 Techniques for Effortless Writing 40

    Stream of Consciousness Writing: Unlocking the Flow of Unfiltered Thoughts 40

    Prompts and Triggers in Automatic Writing. 45

    Guided Writing Exercises 50

    Meditation and Mindfulness: Cultivating Inner Presence and Tranquility 56

Chapter 4 Overcoming Writer's Block 61

    Identifying and Addressing Writer's Blocks 61

    Using Automatic Writing to Break Through Writer's Block 66

    Building Consistency in Your Writing Practice 70

Chapter 5 Exploring Creativity Through Automatic Writing 76

    Connecting with Your Inner Creativity 76

    Unleashing Your Imagination 82

    Tapping into Your Subconscious Mind 87

Chapter 6 Practical Applications 93

    Journaling and Self-Reflection 93

    Understanding Creative Writing and Fiction 98

    Problem Solving and Decision Making 103

    Personal Growth and Healing 108

Chapter 7 Ethical Considerations 115

    Privacy and Personal Boundaries: Nurturing Healthy Relationships and Well-Being 115

    The Ethical Use of Automatic Writing 120

    Respect for Others' Privacy 125

Chapter 8 Advanced Techniques 130

    Automatic Writing with Tarot or Oracle Cards 130

    Channeling and Spiritual Guidance 135

    Collaborative Writing with Your Subconscious: Unleashing Creativity and Insight 139

Conclusion 146

    The Transformative Power of Automatic Writing 146

    Encouragement and Final Thoughts 150

Introduction

In a world filled with distractions, responsibilities, and the ceaseless hustle and bustle of everyday life, finding the time and inspiration to engage in creative writing can often feel like an insurmountable challenge. As aspiring writers and seasoned authors alike grapple with writer's block, self-doubt, and the ever-elusive muse, the act of putting pen to paper (or fingers to keyboard) can become a source of frustration rather than a channel for self-expression and creativity.

But what if there was a way to make the act of writing effortless? What if you could tap into a wellspring of inspiration that flows effortlessly from your mind to the page? What if, instead of wrestling with your inner critic, you could effortlessly unlock your creative potential and watch your words flow like a river?

This is the promise and power of automatic writing.

Automatic writing is a fascinating and transformative practice that has been used by writers, artists, and thinkers throughout history to access their innermost thoughts, ideas, and creativity. It is a technique that allows you to bypass the conscious mind and connect with the deep well of your subconscious, where creativity, intuition, and untapped potential reside.

In this book, we will explore the art and science of automatic writing, demystifying its history, techniques, and benefits. We will guide you through the process of preparing for automatic writing, provide you with a range of powerful writing exercises and prompts, and help you overcome common challenges like writer's block and self-doubt.

"The Effortless Pen: Unlocking Creativity with Automatic Writing Tools" is designed as your comprehensive guide to harnessing the transformative power of automatic writing. Whether you're a seasoned writer looking to break free from creative ruts or someone entirely new to the world of writing, this book offers something valuable for everyone.

In the chapters that follow, we will:

Define automatic writing and its historical context, shedding light on its origins and evolution.

Explore the many benefits of automatic writing, from boosting creativity and problem-solving to enhancing personal growth and self-awareness.

Provide practical advice on creating the ideal writing space, choosing the right tools, and setting intentions for your writing practice.

Offer a diverse range of automatic writing techniques, from stream of consciousness writing to guided exercises, meditation, and mindfulness practices.

Share tips and strategies for overcoming common obstacles and challenges that may arise during your automatic writing journey.

Discuss ethical considerations when using automatic writing, emphasizing the importance of respecting your own boundaries and the privacy of others.

Dive into advanced techniques like combining automatic writing with tarot or oracle cards, channeling, and collaborative writing with your subconscious.

Provide troubleshooting guidance and offer ways to integrate automatic writing into your daily life for long-term benefits.

By the time you finish reading this book, you'll not only understand the theory and practice of automatic writing but also have the tools and confidence to embark on your own effortless writing journey. Whether your goal is to enhance your creativity, find solutions to life's challenges, or simply enjoy the joy of self-expression, automatic writing can be your key to unlocking the limitless potential of your inner world.

So, grab your pen and paper (or your favorite writing device), and let's embark on this transformative journey together. The pages that follow hold the keys to unlocking your creativity and discovering the magic of "The Effortless Pen."

Chapter 1
Understanding Automatic Writing

In this chapter, we delve into the fundamentals of automatic writing. We define what automatic writing is and provide insights into its historical significance. You'll gain a clear understanding of the benefits it offers and dispel common misconceptions about this intriguing practice.

What Is Automatic Writing?

Automatic writing is a remarkable and often misunderstood practice that serves as a powerful gateway to the depths of the human mind. It is a process through which individuals allow their subconscious thoughts, ideas, and creativity to flow onto paper or screen without the interference of conscious thought. This seemingly mystical technique has fascinated writers, artists, and thinkers for centuries, offering a unique channel for self-expression, exploration, and creativity.

Historical Origins and Evolution

The origins of automatic writing can be traced back to the late 19th century when it gained prominence as a method for communicating with the spirit world. Spiritualists and mediums claimed that during séances, they would enter a trance-like state and write messages or produce artworks purportedly guided by spirits or entities from the beyond. This spiritual aspect of automatic writing gave it an aura of mysticism and led to its association with the paranormal.

However, it's important to note that automatic writing has a much older history in various cultures around the world. It can be found in practices like shamanic journeying, divination, and visionary experiences. Indigenous cultures and ancient civilizations often used similar techniques to access the wisdom of the subconscious mind.

Over time, automatic writing evolved beyond its spiritual and mystical associations. Psychologists and scholars began to study it as a psychological phenomenon. Sigmund Freud, the renowned psychoanalyst, explored the concept of "free association," a process similar to automatic writing, as a means to access the unconscious mind and uncover repressed thoughts and emotions.

In contemporary times, automatic writing has taken on a more secular and therapeutic role. It is widely used as a tool for personal growth, creativity enhancement, problem-solving, and self-reflection. Writers, artists, and individuals seeking self-discovery have embraced automatic writing as a way to tap into their inner worlds.

The Process of Automatic Writing

At its core, automatic writing involves bypassing the critical and analytical functions of the conscious mind to allow the subconscious to express itself freely. Here's a simplified overview of the process:

Preparation: To begin, find a quiet and comfortable space where you won't be easily distracted. Have your writing tools ready—whether it's pen and paper or a computer.

Setting Intentions: Setting a clear intention is essential. You might wish to gain insights, solve a specific problem, or simply explore your creativity. This intention will guide your session.

Relaxation: Take a few moments to relax and clear your mind. Some people use meditation or deep breathing exercises to achieve this state.

Start Writing: Begin writing without consciously thinking about what you're going to say. Let the words flow naturally. Don't worry about grammar, punctuation, or coherence at this stage.

Suspend Judgment: Avoid analyzing or critiquing what you're writing. The goal is to let go of the conscious mind's control and allow the subconscious to express itself without hindrance.

Review and Reflect: Once you feel your writing session is complete, take a step back. Read what you've written and reflect on the content. You may discover insights, emotions, or ideas that you weren't consciously aware of.

Benefits of Automatic Writing

Automatic writing offers a wide range of benefits, making it a versatile tool for personal and creative exploration:

Creativity Enhancement: By tapping into the subconscious, automatic writing can unlock a wellspring of creativity. It's a valuable resource for writers, artists, and anyone seeking innovative solutions.

Self-Discovery: Through automatic writing, individuals can gain deeper insights into their thoughts, feelings, and beliefs. It can help uncover hidden desires, fears, and unresolved issues.

Problem-Solving: Many use automatic writing to tackle complex problems or make difficult decisions. The unfiltered nature of the subconscious often leads to fresh perspectives and solutions.

Stress Reduction: Engaging in automatic writing can be a therapeutic way to relieve stress and anxiety. It provides a safe space to express and process emotions.

Enhanced Intuition: As you become more attuned to your subconscious through regular practice, your intuition can sharpen, helping you make better choices in various aspects of life.

Artistic Expression: Artists often use automatic drawing or writing to create unique and abstract artworks that reflect the depths of their minds.

Common Misconceptions about Automatic Writing

Automatic writing is not without its misconceptions, many of which arise from its historical association with the paranormal. Here are a few key misconceptions dispelled:

Spiritual Communication: While automatic writing was historically linked to spirit communication, it doesn't necessarily involve contact with otherworldly entities. It's primarily a means of accessing your own subconscious.

Lack of Control: Some fear that automatic writing leads to a loss of control or opens the door to negative influences. In reality, you remain in control during the process and can stop at any time.

Automatic Writing as a Cure-All: Automatic writing is a valuable tool, but it's not a magical solution to all problems. It requires practice and may not work for everyone.

In conclusion, automatic writing is a fascinating practice that invites you to explore the depths of your own mind. Its historical roots in spiritualism have given way to a modern, secular approach focused on personal growth, creativity, and self-discovery. As you embark on your own journey of automatic writing, you'll uncover the hidden treasures of your subconscious and unlock the limitless potential of your inner world.

Historical Perspective of Automatic Writing

The practice of automatic writing, though often associated with the 19th-century spiritualist movement, has a much richer historical tapestry that spans cultures and centuries. This intriguing phenomenon, which involves writing without conscious thought, can be traced back to ancient civilizations and has evolved through various stages, reflecting the changing beliefs and understandings of different eras.

Ancient Beginnings

The roots of automatic writing can be found in the mystical and spiritual practices of ancient cultures. In many civilizations, scribes and shamans would enter altered states of consciousness through rituals, meditation, or trance-inducing techniques to access hidden knowledge or communicate with deities and spirits. These altered states often led to spontaneous writing or drawing that was believed to be divinely inspired.

In ancient Greece, the Oracle at Delphi is a famous example. The Pythia, the priestess of Apollo, would enter a trance-like state and utter prophetic words that were transcribed by scribes. This divinely inspired utterance bears a resemblance to the concept of automatic writing, where the writer becomes a conduit for messages from the subconscious or higher realms.

Similarly, various indigenous cultures around the world practiced forms of trance writing or drawing as a means of connecting with the spiritual realm, seeking guidance, and preserving their cultural heritage. These practices were often deeply intertwined with their belief systems and rituals.

Spiritualism and the 19th Century

The 19th century saw a resurgence of interest in spiritualism, a movement centered around the belief in communication with the spirit world. During this period, automatic writing gained prominence as a method for purportedly channeling messages from the deceased. Spiritualists and mediums claimed that they could enter a trance state and write messages or create artwork under the guidance of spirits.

One of the most famous cases of automatic writing during this era was that of the Fox sisters, who were credited with initiating the modern spiritualist movement. In 1848, the sisters claimed to communicate with a spirit through a series of raps and knocks. This led to a wave of interest in mediumship and spirit communication, including automatic writing sessions.

Authors and intellectuals of the time, such as Arthur Conan Doyle and William James, became involved in exploring psychic phenomena, including automatic writing. They conducted investigations and documented cases of automatic writing, contributing to its popularity and acceptance.

Psychological Exploration

As the 19th century turned into the 20th century, the field of psychology began to emerge and shed new light on the phenomenon of automatic writing. Sigmund Freud, the father of psychoanalysis, explored a similar concept known as "free association." This technique involved patients saying whatever came to mind without censorship to access the unconscious and reveal repressed thoughts and emotions.

Freud's work and the development of psychology as a discipline brought a more scientific perspective to automatic writing. It was no longer solely seen as a channel for spiritual messages but as a process rooted in the workings of the human mind.

Modern Perspectives and Applications

In the modern era, automatic writing has evolved beyond its spiritualist and psychoanalytic roots. It has become a versatile tool used for various purposes, including personal growth, creativity enhancement, and problem-solving. Writers, artists, and individuals seeking self-discovery have embraced it as a way to tap into their inner worlds.

Therapists sometimes use automatic writing as a therapeutic technique to help clients explore their thoughts and emotions, particularly when dealing with trauma or inner conflicts. It can provide a safe and non-judgmental space for self-expression and reflection.

Many authors and artists incorporate automatic writing into their creative processes. By bypassing the critical and self-censoring conscious mind, they access a wellspring of inspiration and produce works that are uniquely unfiltered by rational thought.

Scientific Exploration

In recent years, scientific research has started to explore the neural mechanisms behind automatic writing. Neuroscientists have used functional MRI (fMRI) and EEG scans to study brain activity during automatic writing sessions. These studies suggest that during automatic writing, there is reduced activity in the prefrontal cortex—the region associated with conscious thought and self-awareness—allowing the subconscious mind to express itself more freely.

Understanding the neuroscience behind automatic writing may open up new avenues for research and applications, such as using it as a therapeutic tool for individuals with certain cognitive or emotional challenges.

The history of automatic writing is a rich tapestry that weaves together elements of spirituality, psychology, and creativity. From its ancient origins in shamanic practices and oracles to its prominence in 19th-century spiritualism and its integration into modern psychology and creative processes, automatic writing has evolved and adapted to the changing beliefs and needs of each era.

Today, it stands as a versatile and valuable tool for personal growth, self-discovery, artistic expression, and even scientific exploration. As our understanding of the human mind continues to deepen, automatic writing remains a fascinating window into the depths of our consciousness, offering a bridge between the conscious and subconscious realms. It is a testament to the enduring human desire to explore the inner workings of our minds and unlock the mysteries of creativity and self-awareness.

Benefits of Automatic Writing

Automatic writing, a practice that involves writing without conscious thought, offers a multitude of benefits that can positively impact various aspects of one's life. While it may seem mysterious or esoteric, the advantages of automatic writing are grounded in psychology, creativity, personal growth, and problem-solving. In this exploration, we will delve into the depth and breadth of these benefits, shedding light on why this practice has gained popularity and remains a powerful tool for those seeking to unlock their inner creativity and insights.

Creativity Enhancement

One of the foremost benefits of automatic writing is its ability to enhance creativity. When you engage in automatic writing, you bypass the critical and analytical functions of the conscious mind, allowing your thoughts and ideas to flow freely. This unfiltered expression often leads to innovative and unexpected insights. Writers, artists, and creative thinkers use automatic writing to break free from creative blocks and access new sources of inspiration.

Creative individuals often find that automatic writing helps them tap into a wellspring of ideas and concepts they might not have consciously considered. It encourages divergent thinking, the ability to explore multiple solutions and perspectives, which is essential for creative problem-solving and artistic expression.

Self-Discovery and Self-Reflection

Automatic writing serves as a mirror to your inner world. It provides a unique opportunity for self-discovery and self-reflection. By allowing your subconscious thoughts to surface, you gain insights into your beliefs, desires, fears, and inner conflicts. This increased self-awareness can lead to personal growth and empowerment.

Many people use automatic writing as a form of journaling, using it to explore their thoughts and emotions in a non-judgmental way. It can be especially helpful for individuals working through difficult experiences, as it offers a safe and private space to express and process their feelings.

Problem-Solving and Decision Making

The process of automatic writing can be a valuable tool for problem-solving and decision-making. When faced with complex challenges or difficult decisions, automatic writing allows you to explore multiple perspectives and potential solutions. By setting an intention related to the problem or decision at hand, you can access your subconscious wisdom and generate insights that may not be apparent through conscious thought alone.

This problem-solving aspect of automatic writing is akin to brainstorming but with the added advantage of accessing deeper layers of your mind. It can lead to innovative solutions and a clearer understanding of the issues you're facing.

Stress Reduction and Emotional Release

Engaging in automatic writing can be a therapeutic way to relieve stress and release pent-up emotions. The act of writing down your thoughts and feelings can serve as a cathartic release, allowing you to process and let go of emotional burdens. It's a form of self-care that provides emotional clarity and promotes mental well-being.

For individuals who struggle with anxiety or overwhelming emotions, automatic writing can be a grounding practice. It helps bring a sense of order to the chaos of thoughts and feelings, providing a sense of control and emotional relief.

Enhanced Intuition

As you become more attuned to your subconscious mind through regular practice, your intuition often becomes sharper. Intuition is the ability to make decisions or sense information without the need for conscious reasoning. Automatic writing can help you develop and trust your intuition, which can be a valuable asset in various aspects of life, from personal relationships to professional endeavors.

Intuitive insights gained through automatic writing can guide you in making choices that align with your deepest desires and values. Many successful individuals credit their intuition as a crucial factor in their decision-making process.

Artistic Expression

Automatic writing is not limited to text; it extends to drawing and other forms of artistic expression. Artists often use automatic drawing or painting as a means to tap into their subconscious creativity. These artworks can be abstract and symbolic, reflecting the depths of the artist's mind in a way that transcends conscious control.

The process of creating art through automatic writing can be both therapeutic and inspirational. It allows artists to connect with their inner visions and produce works that are deeply personal and evocative.

Spiritual and Mindful Practice

For those on a spiritual or mindful journey, automatic writing can serve as a powerful practice for connecting with higher consciousness, exploring one's spirituality, and seeking answers to existential questions. It can be a form of meditation in which you become a conduit for spiritual guidance or insights.

By setting a spiritual intention and surrendering to the process, individuals often report a sense of deep connection, inner peace, and a heightened sense of purpose through their automatic writing sessions.

Enhanced Communication Skills

Improving one's communication skills is another valuable benefit of automatic writing. By practicing the free flow of thoughts and ideas onto paper, you become more adept at expressing yourself coherently and effectively. This can translate into better verbal communication, writing, and even public speaking.

Furthermore, enhanced communication skills can lead to improved relationships, both personally and professionally. Clearer and more authentic communication fosters understanding and connection with others.

Diary of Insights and Inspiration

Automatic writing can serve as a diary of insights and inspiration. Over time, as you engage in regular sessions, you accumulate a treasure trove of ideas, thoughts, and reflections. These writings can become a valuable resource that you can revisit whenever you need guidance, inspiration, or a reminder of your personal growth journey.

Enhanced Goal Setting and Achievement

By tapping into your subconscious mind through automatic writing, you can gain clarity on your goals and aspirations. This clarity is a powerful tool for setting and achieving your objectives. Whether it's personal goals like self-improvement or professional goals like career advancement, automatic writing can help you define your path and identify the steps needed to reach your desired outcomes.

In conclusion, the benefits of automatic writing are far-reaching and deeply transformative. This practice provides a pathway to creativity, self-discovery, problem-solving, stress reduction, enhanced intuition, artistic expression, spiritual connection, improved communication, and goal achievement. As you explore and integrate automatic writing into your life, you open the door to a wealth of insights and possibilities that can enrich your personal and creative journey. Whether you're a writer seeking inspiration or an individual on a quest for self-understanding, automatic writing can be a guiding light, illuminating the depths of your inner world.

Common Misconceptions About Automatic Writing: Separating Fact from Fiction

Automatic writing, a practice in which individuals allow their subconscious thoughts to flow onto paper or a screen without conscious control, is often shrouded in mystery and misunderstanding. These misconceptions can deter people from exploring this valuable tool for creativity, self-discovery, and problem-solving. In this exploration, we will debunk some of the most common misconceptions about automatic writing, shedding light on what it truly entails and its potential benefits.

Misconception 1: Automatic Writing Involves Contact with the Spirit World

One of the most persistent misconceptions about automatic writing is that it involves communication with the spirit world or entities from beyond. While automatic writing has historical ties to spiritualism, where mediums claimed to channel spirits, it doesn't necessarily involve supernatural contact.

Fact: Automatic writing primarily involves tapping into your own subconscious mind. It is a process that allows you to access your thoughts, feelings, and creativity without the interference of conscious thought. While some practitioners may use it as a form of spiritual or intuitive guidance, it's not inherently tied to communicating with external entities. Instead, it's a tool for introspection and self-expression.

Misconception 2: You Lose Control During Automatic Writing

Another misconception is that engaging in automatic writing leads to a loss of control or surrendering one's will to external forces.

Fact: When you practice automatic writing, you remain in control. You set the intention for your session, and you can start or stop the process at any time. It's more akin to entering a focused and receptive state of mind rather than losing control. You are still the author of the content and have the agency to decide what to do with it.

Misconception 3: Automatic Writing Is a Cure-All for All Problems

Some people believe that automatic writing is a magical solution to all life's problems, providing instant answers and solutions.

Fact: Automatic writing is a valuable tool, but it's not a panacea. It's not guaranteed to provide immediate solutions or insights for every challenge you face. Its effectiveness depends on various factors, including your level of practice, the clarity of your intention, and the specific issue you're addressing. It's a process that may require patience and consistency to yield meaningful results.

Misconception 4: Automatic Writing Is Only for Writers or Artists

There's a common misconception that automatic writing is exclusively for writers or artists seeking creative inspiration.

Fact: While automatic writing can certainly benefit writers and artists by enhancing creativity, it is not limited to these groups. Anyone can practice automatic writing, regardless of their creative or professional background. It is a versatile tool for personal growth, self-reflection, problem-solving, and gaining insights into various aspects of life.

Misconception 5: Automatic Writing Is Incomprehensible or Chaotic

Some believe that automatic writing results in incomprehensible or chaotic scribbles that have no meaning.

Fact: While the initial output of automatic writing may appear disjointed or abstract, it often contains valuable insights and symbolism that can be deciphered with reflection. The apparent chaos is the result of bypassing the conscious mind's filter, allowing the raw thoughts and feelings of the subconscious to surface. With practice and analysis, you can extract meaning and coherence from your automatic writing.

Misconception 6: You Must Have Exceptional Writing Skills

There's a misconception that you need exceptional writing skills or a strong command of language to engage in automatic writing effectively.

Fact: Automatic writing does not require exceptional writing skills. In fact, it's not about producing polished prose or following grammatical rules. The focus is on the content and the process of allowing your thoughts to flow freely. It's a practice of self-expression, and the quality of the writing is secondary to the insights and ideas it uncovers.

Misconception 7: It's a Rapid Process with Immediate Results

Some believe that automatic writing should yield immediate and rapid results, providing instant answers or profound insights.

Fact: While automatic writing can yield quick insights, it's not always an instant process. The depth and clarity of the content can vary from session to session. Some sessions may produce immediate insights, while others may require more time and practice to reveal meaningful information. Patience and persistence are key to harnessing its full potential.

Misconception 8: Automatic Writing Is Limited to Text

Another misconception is that automatic writing is limited to text and cannot extend to other forms of creative expression.

Fact: Automatic writing can manifest in various forms, including drawings, paintings, and other visual arts. Automatic drawing, for example, is a practice where individuals let their hand move freely across a canvas or paper, producing abstract or symbolic artwork. This form of expression allows artists to tap into their subconscious creativity beyond the written word.

Misconception 9: It's a One-Size-Fits-All Practice

Some people assume that there is a single, standardized way to practice automatic writing that works for everyone.

Fact: Automatic writing is a flexible and adaptable practice. There is no one-size-fits-all approach. The techniques and methods may vary from person to person. What works best for you may differ from what works for someone else. It's essential to experiment and find the approach that aligns with your intentions and goals.

Misconception 10: It Requires Special Equipment or Materials

There's a misconception that you need special equipment or materials to engage in automatic writing effectively.

Fact: Automatic writing can be practiced with basic materials such as pen and paper or a simple computer word processor. There is no need for expensive or specialized equipment. The focus should be on the practice itself, not the tools you use.

In conclusion, automatic writing is a valuable and versatile practice with numerous benefits, but it is often clouded by common misconceptions. By dispelling these myths, we can encourage individuals to explore automatic writing with an open mind, understanding that it is a personal journey of self-discovery, creativity, and growth. It offers a unique opportunity to connect with the subconscious mind and unlock the hidden treasures of one's inner world, free from the constraints of preconceived notions.

Chapter 2
Preparing for Automatic Writing

In this chapter, we'll lay the groundwork for your automatic writing journey. Preparation is key to a successful practice. We'll guide you through creating an ideal writing space, choosing the right tools and materials, setting intentions for your sessions, and clearing your mind to ensure a productive and meaningful experience.

Creating a Writing Space for Automatic Writing: Cultivating the Ideal Environment

The practice of automatic writing, which involves tapping into the subconscious mind to express thoughts and ideas freely, benefits greatly from the creation of a conducive and inspiring writing space. Your environment can significantly influence the quality and depth of your automatic writing sessions. In this exploration, we will delve into the elements of crafting an ideal writing space that encourages focus, creativity, and a deep connection with your inner thoughts.

Choose a Quiet and Distraction-Free Location

Selecting the right location for your writing space is paramount. It should be a quiet and distraction-free area where you can immerse yourself fully in the practice. Consider the following:

Privacy: Ensure that your writing space provides privacy, especially if you intend to explore personal or sensitive topics during your automatic writing sessions. Privacy can help you feel more comfortable and secure in expressing your thoughts.

Minimal Distractions: Minimize external distractions such as noisy surroundings, electronic devices, or interruptions from others. The fewer distractions present, the easier it will be to enter a focused and receptive state of mind.

Natural Light: Whenever possible, choose a location with access to natural light. Natural light not only enhances your mood but also provides a clear and well-lit workspace, reducing eye strain.

Arrange Comfortable Seating

Your choice of seating is crucial for maintaining comfort and focus during automatic writing sessions. Consider the following factors:

Comfort: Select a comfortable chair or cushion that supports your posture and allows you to sit for an extended period without discomfort. An ergonomic chair can be an excellent investment for long writing sessions.

Back Support: Ensure that your seating provides adequate back support to prevent discomfort or strain. Proper alignment can enhance your concentration and prevent physical distractions.

Adequate Workspace: Arrange your seating in a way that provides ample workspace for your writing materials, whether it's a desk, table, or lap desk. A clutter-free workspace promotes a clear and organized mind.

Personalize Your Space

Creating a writing space that feels personal and inspiring can enhance your connection with the practice of automatic writing. Consider the following personalization tips:

Decor and Aesthetics: Decorate your writing space with items that resonate with you. These could include artwork, photographs, inspirational quotes, or symbols that hold personal significance. Surrounding yourself with meaningful objects can create a sense of comfort and motivation.

Sensory Elements: Engage multiple senses to foster a deeper connection with your space. Incorporate scents, such as candles or essential oils, that promote relaxation or focus. Soft background music or ambient sounds can enhance the ambiance.

Personal Rituals: Establishing a simple ritual before your automatic writing sessions can help signal your mind that it's time to transition into a receptive state. Lighting a candle, taking a few deep breaths, or setting an intention can be part of your personal ritual.

Organize Your Writing Tools and Materials

Efficiency in automatic writing is closely tied to how well-organized your writing tools and materials are. A well-organized workspace can save time and reduce frustration. Consider the following organization tips:

Writing Implements: Ensure that you have an adequate supply of pens, pencils, or other writing tools that you prefer. Avoid interruptions during your sessions by having extra writing materials nearby.

Notebooks or Paper: If you're using paper, have a stack of clean sheets or notebooks at the ready. Organize them neatly within arm's reach to avoid disruptions while searching for new pages.

Technology: If you prefer digital writing tools, have your computer, tablet, or smartphone prepared and free of notifications that may distract you during your sessions.

Mindful Lighting and Ambiance

The lighting and overall ambiance of your writing space can significantly impact your mindset and focus. Consider the following tips:

Lighting: Opt for lighting that is comfortable and conducive to concentration. Soft, warm lighting can create a cozy atmosphere, while natural light during the day can be invigorating. Avoid harsh or overly bright lighting that can cause eye strain.

Ambiance: Set the tone with elements that create a soothing and focused ambiance. Plants, artwork, or calming color schemes can contribute to a serene and inspiring atmosphere.

Maintain Cleanliness and Order

A cluttered or disorganized workspace can be distracting and hinder your ability to focus during automatic writing sessions. Regularly maintain cleanliness and order in your writing space by:

Decluttering: Periodically review and declutter your workspace. Remove any unnecessary items that may accumulate over time.

Organization: Use storage solutions such as shelves, drawers, or containers to keep your writing materials organized and easily accessible.

Cleanliness: Keep your workspace clean and dust-free. A tidy environment promotes mental clarity and calm.

Set an Intention for Your Space

Infuse your writing space with intention by defining its purpose and the energy you wish to cultivate during your automatic writing sessions. Consider the following:

Intention Statement: Craft a simple intention statement for your writing space, such as "This space is where I connect with my inner wisdom and creativity." Repeating this intention before each session can reinforce its purpose.

Symbols or Tokens: Place symbols or tokens that represent your intention in your writing space. These could be objects associated with your goals, such as a small statue or a meaningful crystal.

Creating an ideal writing space for automatic writing is a mindful and intentional process. By carefully selecting your environment, personalizing it to reflect your unique preferences and intentions, and maintaining its cleanliness and order, you can establish a sanctuary for deep exploration of your inner thoughts and creativity. Your writing space becomes a supportive partner in your automatic writing journey, enhancing your ability to access the treasures of your subconscious mind and facilitating meaningful self-discovery.

Tools and Materials for Automatic Writing: Equipping Yourself for Creative Exploration

To embark on a successful journey of automatic writing, it's essential to choose the right tools and materials. These elements can significantly influence the quality and ease of your sessions. Whether you prefer the tactile experience of pen and paper or the convenience of digital platforms, the right tools and materials can enhance your connection with your subconscious mind and facilitate a productive and meaningful automatic writing practice. In this exploration, we will delve into the various options and considerations for selecting the tools and materials that best suit your preferences and goals.

Traditional Pen and Paper

For many practitioners, the classic combination of a pen or pencil and paper remains the preferred choice for automatic writing. The tactile sensation of writing on paper can create a more intimate connection with your thoughts and emotions. Here's what to consider when using this traditional method:

Pen or Pencil: Choose a pen or pencil that feels comfortable in your hand and glides smoothly on paper. The right writing instrument can make a significant difference in your writing experience.

Paper: Select high-quality, unlined paper or a notebook that you enjoy writing on. Some individuals prefer blank pages, while others may find comfort in ruled or grid-lined paper.

Journal: Consider dedicating a specific journal or notebook to your automatic writing practice. This journal can serve as a repository for your thoughts and insights over time, allowing you to track your progress and personal growth.

Accessories: You may also want to include accessories such as bookmarks, sticky notes, or tabs to help you organize and revisit specific entries or insights.

Digital Writing Tools

In an increasingly digital world, many practitioners turn to digital devices and applications for their automatic writing sessions. Digital tools offer convenience, portability, and the ability to easily save and organize your writings. Here's what to consider when using digital writing tools:

Laptop or Tablet: A laptop, tablet, or even a smartphone can serve as your digital writing device. Choose one with a comfortable keyboard or touchscreen interface that suits your preferences.

Writing Software or Apps: Explore writing software or apps that allow you to create, edit, and save your writings. Many word processing applications offer distraction-free writing modes to enhance focus.

Cloud Storage: Consider using cloud storage solutions to store and synchronize your writings across devices. This ensures that your work is accessible wherever and whenever you need it.

Backup: Implement a reliable backup system to safeguard your digital writings. Regularly save your work and consider using external hard drives or online backup services.

Writing Implements for Personalization

Your choice of writing implements can add a personal touch to your automatic writing practice. Here are some options to consider:

Fountain Pen: If you appreciate the artistry and tradition of writing, a fountain pen may be a delightful choice. The smooth flow of ink and the character of each stroke can enhance the writing experience.

Calligraphy Pens: Calligraphy pens come in various styles and nib sizes, allowing you to experiment with different writing aesthetics. They can add artistic flair to your automatic writing.

Markers or Colored Pens: Introducing colored markers or pens can infuse your automatic writing with creativity and symbolism. You can use colors to represent different emotions, themes, or ideas.

Fine-Tip Pens: Fine-tip pens or micro pens offer precision and are ideal for individuals who prefer a clean and controlled writing style.

Setting the Mood with Materials

Creating a conducive atmosphere for automatic writing can involve materials that set the mood and enhance your connection with your inner thoughts. Consider these options:

Candles: Scented or unscented candles can provide a soothing ambiance. Lighting a candle before your session can be part of your pre-writing ritual.

Incense or Essential Oils: Aromatherapy can influence your mindset and focus. Select scents that promote relaxation, clarity, or creativity to enhance your writing space.

Crystals: Crystals and gemstones are believed to have unique energies and properties. Placing specific crystals, such as amethyst for intuition or rose quartz for self-love, near your writing area can amplify your intentions.

Soundscapes: Ambient sounds or calming music can create a tranquil atmosphere. Nature sounds, instrumental music, or binaural beats can help you enter a receptive state of mind.

Additional Tools for Inspiration

Depending on your goals and preferences, you may want to incorporate additional tools and materials that inspire and support your automatic writing practice:

Oracle or Tarot Cards: Some practitioners use oracle or tarot cards as prompts for their automatic writing sessions. Drawing a card before writing can provide a theme or focus for your session.

Mindfulness Tools: Mindfulness exercises, such as meditation cushions, singing bowls, or mindfulness apps, can help you enter a centered and focused state before writing.

Art Supplies: If you enjoy combining art with writing, consider having art supplies like watercolors, colored pencils, or sketchbooks available for spontaneous creative expression.

Reference Books: Keep books or references related to your interests, whether it's symbolism, dream interpretation, or personal development, within reach to inspire your writing.

Regular Maintenance and Cleaning

Regardless of the tools and materials you choose, it's essential to maintain and clean them regularly. Pens should be checked for ink levels and cleaned as needed, while digital devices should be kept in good working condition. A clean and well-maintained writing space promotes focus and minimizes distractions.

In conclusion, selecting the right tools and materials for your automatic writing practice is a personal choice that should align with your preferences and goals. Whether you opt for the tactile experience of traditional pen and paper, the convenience of digital writing tools, or a combination of both, the key is to create an environment that encourages your connection with your inner thoughts and emotions. Your choice of writing implements and materials can add depth, creativity, and personalization to your practice, enhancing the overall experience of automatic writing and helping you unlock the treasures of your subconscious mind.

Setting Intentions for Your Automatic Writing Practice: Guiding Your Inner Journey

Setting intentions is a fundamental step in any meaningful endeavor, and automatic writing is no exception. Intentions provide purpose and direction, shaping the focus and outcomes of your sessions. Whether you are seeking creative inspiration, self-discovery, problem-solving, or personal growth, clearly defined intentions can help guide your inner journey and make your automatic writing practice more fulfilling and purposeful. In this exploration, we will delve into the art of setting intentions for your automatic writing sessions, offering insights and techniques to enhance your practice.

Understanding the Power of Intentions

Intentions are like compasses that orient you in the direction you want to go. They serve as roadmaps for your subconscious mind, guiding it toward specific goals or outcomes. When you set intentions for your automatic writing practice, you activate your mind's natural capacity to focus on what matters most to you. This focus is essential for channeling your thoughts, emotions, and creativity in a purposeful way.

Intentions also serve as a bridge between your conscious and subconscious minds. They allow you to communicate your desires, questions, or areas of exploration to your inner self. By stating your intentions clearly, you invite your subconscious to collaborate with your conscious awareness, creating a powerful synergy that can yield profound insights and outcomes.

Types of Intentions for Automatic Writing

Intentions for automatic writing can be diverse, reflecting your unique goals and interests. Here are some common types of intentions:

Creativity and Inspiration: If your primary goal is to enhance your creative output or find inspiration for artistic or writing projects, your intention might be to access new ideas, overcome creative blocks, or unlock your creative potential.

Self-Discovery and Personal Growth: Intentions related to self-discovery may involve exploring your inner thoughts, emotions, and beliefs. You might aim to gain clarity about your values, understand past experiences, or identify areas for personal growth and development.

Problem-Solving: When using automatic writing for problem-solving, your intention could be to find solutions to specific challenges or dilemmas. You might seek insights into a personal or professional issue, allowing your subconscious to provide fresh perspectives.

Emotional Release and Healing: If you're using automatic writing as a therapeutic tool, your intention may revolve around releasing pent-up emotions, processing trauma, or achieving emotional healing and balance.

Spiritual Exploration: Individuals on a spiritual journey may set intentions to connect with their higher selves, seek guidance from a higher power, or explore existential questions. These intentions often invite deeper spiritual insights and experiences.

Daily Reflection and Gratitude: Some people use automatic writing as a daily practice for reflection and gratitude. Their intentions might involve starting or ending the day with a clear mind, expressing gratitude for life's blessings, or setting positive intentions for the day ahead.

Intuitive Guidance: Intentions for intuitive guidance focus on receiving insights or guidance from your inner wisdom or intuition. You might seek answers to pressing questions or seek direction in areas of uncertainty.

How to Set Effective Intentions

Effective intentions are specific, clear, and aligned with your true desires and goals. Here are steps to help you set effective intentions for your automatic writing practice:

Reflect on Your Goals: Take time to reflect on your overarching goals and what you hope to achieve through automatic writing. Are you seeking personal insight, creative inspiration, problem-solving, or emotional healing? Clarify your primary goal.

Be Specific: Make your intention as specific as possible. Instead of a vague goal like "find answers," consider a more specific intention like "gain clarity on my career path" or "uncover the root cause of my anxiety."

Use Positive Language: Frame your intention in positive language. Instead of saying "stop feeling anxious," phrase it as "cultivate inner peace and emotional balance." Positive intentions are more empowering and motivating.

State Your Intention Clearly: Write down your intention in a clear and concise sentence. The act of writing it down reinforces your commitment to it. For example, "I intend to receive insights into my creative project's direction."

Visualize the Outcome: Take a moment to visualize the desired outcome of your automatic writing session. Imagine yourself achieving your intention and how it would positively impact your life.

Invoke Emotion: Feel the emotion associated with your intention as you set it. Emotional resonance adds depth and power to your intention. Connect with the feelings of excitement, clarity, or healing that your intention represents.

Trust Your Inner Wisdom: Trust that your subconscious mind is a wellspring of wisdom and creativity. Approach your automatic writing practice with an open heart and an attitude of curiosity and trust in your inner guidance.

Techniques for Reinforcing Intentions

Reinforcing your intentions can enhance their effectiveness and ensure that they remain at the forefront of your automatic writing practice. Here are techniques to reinforce your intentions:

Mindful Affirmations: Begin your automatic writing sessions with mindful affirmations that reiterate your intention. Repeat your intention as a positive affirmation to set the tone for your session.

Create a Ritual: Develop a pre-writing ritual that aligns with your intention. Lighting a candle, taking a few deep breaths, or engaging in a brief meditation can help you transition into a receptive state of mind.

Journal Your Intentions: Keep a separate journal or section in your automatic writing journal dedicated to your intentions. Write down your intentions before each session to reaffirm your commitment.

Review and Reflect: After your automatic writing session, take a moment to review what you've written and reflect on how it aligns with your intention. This reflection can deepen your understanding and insights.

Visual Aids: Consider creating visual aids or vision boards that represent your intentions. Placing these visuals in your writing space can serve as constant reminders.

Setting intentions for your automatic writing practice is like setting sail on an inner journey. Your intentions act as your compass, guiding you through the uncharted waters of your subconscious mind. With clear and well-defined intentions, you can navigate this inner landscape with purpose and curiosity, uncovering treasures of creativity, self-discovery, and personal growth along the way. As you embark on your automatic writing journey, remember that intentions are not rigid; they can evolve and adapt as you grow and learn from your practice. Trust in the power of intention to illuminate your path and make your automatic writing practice a fulfilling and transformative experience.

Clearing Your Mind.

Clearing your mind is a crucial step in preparing for successful automatic writing sessions. The practice of automatic writing requires a receptive and focused state of mind, free from distractions and cluttered thoughts. By cultivating inner stillness, you create a mental space where your subconscious thoughts can flow freely onto the page. In this exploration, we will delve into the techniques and strategies to help you clear your mind effectively, making your automatic writing practice more productive and insightful.

Understanding the Importance of a Clear Mind

A clear mind is like a blank canvas, ready to receive the brush strokes of your inner thoughts and emotions. It allows you to access the depths of your subconscious without interference from the noise and distractions of everyday life. Here's why clearing your mind is essential for successful automatic writing:

Enhanced Receptivity: A clutter-free mind is more receptive to intuitive insights, creative ideas, and deep self-reflection.

When your mental landscape is clear, you become a more open channel for your inner wisdom to emerge.

Focus and Concentration: Clearing your mind sharpens your focus and concentration. It helps you stay present during your writing sessions, enabling you to explore your thoughts and emotions with clarity and depth.

Reduced Distractions: A cluttered mind is easily distracted by worries, anxieties, or external concerns. Clearing your mind reduces these distractions, allowing you to immerse yourself fully in the practice of automatic writing.

Heightened Creativity: Inner stillness often precedes moments of creative insight. When your mind is clear, you can tap into your creative potential and access novel ideas and solutions.

Emotional Balance: Automatic writing can delve into deep emotional territory. A clear mind provides a stable foundation for processing emotions and gaining insights into your emotional landscape.

Techniques for Clearing Your Mind

Clearing your mind is a skill that can be developed through practice and patience. Here are techniques to help you cultivate inner stillness before your automatic writing sessions:

Meditation: Meditation is a powerful practice for calming the mind and cultivating inner stillness. Dedicate a few minutes before your writing session to meditation. Focus on your breath, a mantra, or a guided meditation that aligns with your intention.

Breath Awareness: Paying attention to your breath is a simple yet effective way to clear your mind. Take slow, deep breaths and observe the rise and fall of your chest or the sensation of air passing through your nostrils. This mindful breathing can anchor your awareness in the present moment.

Progressive Muscle Relaxation: Progressive muscle relaxation involves systematically tensing and relaxing different muscle groups in your body. This practice helps release physical tension and creates a sense of calmness that extends to the mind.

Mindful Body Scan: Conduct a mindful body scan, where you focus your attention on each part of your body, from your toes to your head. This practice increases awareness of bodily sensations and promotes relaxation.

Journaling: Before your writing session, you can engage in journaling as a way to release any cluttered thoughts or emotions. Write down any worries, distractions, or concerns to acknowledge and release them.

Visualization: Visualization techniques involve creating mental imagery that promotes relaxation and clarity. Imagine a peaceful scene, like a serene beach or a tranquil forest, and immerse yourself in the sensory details of this mental sanctuary.

Soundscapes: Use soothing sounds or music to create a calming atmosphere. Nature sounds, ambient music, or binaural beats can help quiet the mind and set the stage for focused writing.

Affirmations: Positive affirmations can help redirect your thoughts and create a positive mindset. Repeating affirmations that resonate with you, such as "I am centered and calm," can be a helpful pre-writing ritual.

Creating a Pre-Writing Ritual

Establishing a pre-writing ritual can signal to your mind that it's time to transition into a clear and focused state. Your ritual can be personalized to suit your preferences and intentions. Here's how to create an effective pre-writing ritual:

Choose a Space: Select a quiet and comfortable space where you will conduct your pre-writing ritual. This space should be dedicated to your automatic writing practice.

Set a Timer: Allocate a specific amount of time for your pre-writing ritual. Depending on your schedule and preferences, it could be anywhere from 5 to 20 minutes.

Mindful Preparation: Begin your ritual with mindfulness. Take a few moments to center yourself by paying attention to your breath or engaging in a short meditation.

Affirmation or Intention: State your intention for the writing session. Use a positive affirmation or mantra that resonates with your goal for the session.

Visualization: Engage in a brief visualization exercise to clear your mind. Imagine a tranquil scene or visualize your creative thoughts flowing freely onto the page.

Breathwork: Focus on your breath for a few minutes, taking slow and deliberate breaths. Inhale calmness and exhale any tension or cluttered thoughts.

Physical Relaxation: If necessary, engage in progressive muscle relaxation or a brief body scan to release physical tension.

Soundscapes: Play calming sounds or music that help you relax and clear your mind.

Journaling: If you have any lingering thoughts or concerns, jot them down in your journal to acknowledge and release them.

Transition to Writing: When your timer signals the end of your pre-writing ritual, transition seamlessly into your automatic writing session. Your mind should now be in a receptive and focused state.

Embracing Patience and Practice

Clearing your mind is not a one-time achievement but an ongoing practice. It's normal for the mind to wander, and distractions may arise. Embrace patience and self-compassion as you continue to refine your ability to clear your mind before automatic writing sessions. With regular practice, you will develop greater mastery over your mental landscape, allowing you to access the profound insights and creative flow that automatic writing can offer. Remember that each session is an opportunity for growth and self-discovery, and every step you take toward inner stillness brings you closer to a more meaningful and transformative automatic writing practice.

Chapter 3
Techniques for Effortless Writing

In this chapter, we'll explore a variety of techniques to make your automatic writing sessions more effortless and productive. These techniques include methods for tapping into your creativity, enhancing your flow of thoughts, overcoming writer's block, and deepening your connection with your inner self. Whether you're a seasoned automatic writer or just starting, these techniques will help you unlock your full potential and make the writing process smoother and more enjoyable.

Stream of Consciousness Writing: Unlocking the Flow of Unfiltered Thoughts

Stream of consciousness writing is a powerful and liberating technique that allows you to tap into the unfiltered flow of your thoughts and emotions. This approach encourages spontaneity and creativity while bypassing the constraints of self-censorship. By embracing the stream of consciousness method, you can access deeper layers of your subconscious mind and gain insights that might otherwise remain hidden. In this exploration, we will delve into the art and benefits of stream of consciousness writing, offering guidance on how to practice it effectively.

Understanding Stream of Consciousness Writing

Stream of consciousness writing, often abbreviated as SOC, is a literary and psychological technique that aims to capture the continuous and unstructured flow of a person's thoughts and feelings as they arise in the mind. It was popularized by writers such as James Joyce, Virginia Woolf, and William Faulkner in the realm of literature, but it has also found application in therapeutic and personal growth contexts.

The essence of stream of consciousness writing lies in allowing your thoughts to pour onto the page without judgment, editing, or premeditation. It's like opening a faucet and letting the thoughts flow freely, regardless of their coherence or rationality. This technique is a departure from structured writing and embraces the chaos and unpredictability of the human mind.

Benefits of Stream of Consciousness Writing

Engaging in stream of consciousness writing offers a range of benefits for personal growth, creativity, and self-expression:

Unearthing Subconscious Insights: SOC allows you to access thoughts and emotions that may reside in your subconscious mind. By giving voice to these hidden aspects of yourself, you can gain insights into your beliefs, fears, desires, and unresolved issues.

Creative Inspiration: Stream of consciousness writing is a powerful tool for artists, writers, and creatives. It can unlock new ideas, perspectives, and storylines that may be buried beneath the surface of your conscious mind.

Stress Reduction: SOC can serve as a form of emotional release. By expressing your thoughts and feelings without restraint, you can alleviate stress, anxiety, and pent-up emotions.

Overcoming Writer's Block: If you're facing writer's block or creative stagnation, SOC can break down mental barriers and kickstart your writing flow.

Enhanced Self-Awareness: Continuous practice of stream of consciousness writing can deepen your self-awareness and help you better understand your thought patterns and emotional responses.

Enhanced Problem Solving: SOC can be used as a problem-solving tool. When faced with a complex issue, you can write down your thoughts and explore potential solutions or insights without filtering your ideas.

How to Practice Stream of Consciousness Writing

Practicing stream of consciousness writing is straightforward, but it requires an open and non-judgmental mindset. Here's a step-by-step guide on how to engage in SOC effectively:

Set Aside Time: Choose a specific time and place for your stream of consciousness writing session. Create an environment where you won't be interrupted or distracted.

Select Your Medium: Decide whether you prefer to write with pen and paper or use a digital platform like a computer or tablet. Choose the medium that feels most comfortable and conducive to free expression.

Set a Timer: To create a sense of structure, set a timer for your session. Start with a manageable duration, such as 10 or 15 minutes, and gradually increase it as you become more comfortable with the practice.

Begin Writing: Start writing without a specific topic or agenda. Let your thoughts flow spontaneously. Don't worry about grammar, punctuation, or coherence. Write whatever comes to mind, even if it seems disjointed or nonsensical.

Keep the Pen Moving: Avoid pausing or hesitating during your writing session. Keep the pen moving or continue typing, even if you're unsure of what to write next. If you encounter a mental block, write "I don't know what to write" or repeat a word until your mind finds a new direction.

Stay Present: Focus on the act of writing and the sensations of putting your thoughts onto the page. Pay attention to the physical act of writing or typing.

Embrace Emotions: Allow your emotions to surface and be expressed through your writing. Don't shy away from discomfort or vulnerability. Embracing your emotions is a key aspect of the stream of consciousness experience.

Refrain from Editing: Avoid the urge to edit or revise what you've written during the session. The goal is to capture the raw, unfiltered stream of your thoughts, so resist the temptation to make corrections.

End Gracefully: When the timer signals the end of your session, conclude gracefully. You can finish with a closing sentence or simply stop writing. Take a moment to reflect on the experience and any insights that emerged.

Review and Reflect: After your session, review what you've written. You may discover unexpected insights, recurring themes, or patterns in your thoughts and emotions. Reflect on the experience and its impact on your mindset.

Tips for Effective Stream of Consciousness Writing

Here are some additional tips to enhance your stream of consciousness writing practice:

Practice Regularly: Consistency is key to reaping the benefits of SOC. Dedicate time for regular sessions, even if they're short. Over time, you'll become more comfortable with the process.

Set an Intention: If you have a specific question or issue you'd like to explore, you can set an intention before your SOC session. This can give your writing a sense of direction without constraining your thoughts.

Use Prompts: If you're struggling to start, consider using prompts to kickstart your stream of consciousness. Prompts can be a word, a phrase, or a question that initiates your writing.

Experiment with Different Mediums: Try writing by hand, typing on a computer, or using voice-to-text software. Different mediums may evoke unique experiences and insights.

Create a Ritual: Develop a pre-writing ritual or set the mood with ambient music or lighting to signal the beginning of your SOC session

Be Patient and Non-Judgmental: SOC may initially feel challenging or disorganized. Be patient with yourself and refrain from self-criticism. Remember that the goal is not perfection but free expression.

Stream of consciousness writing is like stepping into the flow of your inner river of thoughts and emotions. It allows you to explore the depths of your psyche, uncover hidden treasures, and tap into your creative wellspring. By practicing SOC regularly, you can cultivate a profound connection with your inner self and harness the boundless creativity and wisdom that reside within. Embrace the spontaneity, chaos, and beauty of your stream of consciousness, and let it carry you on a journey of self-discovery and self-expression.

Prompts and Triggers in Automatic Writing.

Prompts and triggers are valuable tools in the practice of automatic writing, serving as catalysts for inspiration, self-reflection, and creative exploration. Whether you're looking to jumpstart your writing flow, delve into specific themes, or navigate emotional terrain, prompts and triggers provide a structured starting point while allowing your subconscious mind to take the lead. In this exploration, we will delve into the significance of prompts and triggers in automatic writing, explore their diverse applications, and provide guidance on how to effectively incorporate them into your practice.

Understanding Prompts and Triggers

Prompts and triggers are external stimuli or cues that initiate and guide your automatic writing session. They can take various forms, such as words, phrases, questions, images, or concepts. The purpose of prompts and triggers is to bypass conscious thought and encourage the unfiltered expression of your subconscious mind.

Here's a breakdown of the key elements

Prompts: Prompts are specific words, sentences, or questions that direct your focus and initiate your writing session. They provide a starting point or theme for your exploration. For example, a prompt could be "Write about a significant childhood memory" or "What does happiness mean to you?"

Triggers: Triggers are more abstract or symbolic than prompts. They can be images, symbols, emotions, or sensory experiences that evoke a particular response or state of mind. For instance, a trigger might be an image of a labyrinth, the feeling of nostalgia, or the scent of freshly baked bread.

The Significance of Prompts and Triggers

Prompts and triggers serve several crucial purposes in automatic writing:

Initiating the Flow: They break through initial resistance or writer's block by providing a clear starting point. This jumpstarts the flow of thoughts and words, helping you move beyond mental obstacles.

Focusing Your Exploration: Prompts and triggers guide your exploration toward specific themes, emotions, or topics of interest. They act as signposts for your subconscious, directing its attention.

Stimulating Creativity: They ignite your creative imagination and encourage novel perspectives. Prompts and triggers can lead to unexpected insights and connections, fostering creative growth.

Deepening Self-Reflection: By addressing prompts and triggers, you engage in self-reflection and introspection. They invite you to explore your thoughts, feelings, memories, and beliefs, fostering self-awareness.

Navigating Emotional Terrain: Prompts and triggers can help you navigate and process complex emotions or unresolved issues. They provide a structured framework for addressing emotional experiences.

Applications of Prompts and Triggers

Prompts and triggers can be applied to a wide range of purposes and goals in automatic writing. Here are some common applications:

Creative Writing: Writers often use prompts and triggers to generate ideas, overcome writer's block, or explore new storylines, characters, or themes.

Personal Growth: Automatic writing with prompts and triggers can aid in personal development by encouraging self-reflection, setting intentions, and exploring personal values and goals.

Emotional Healing: Writing with prompts and triggers can be therapeutic, helping individuals process trauma, grief, or emotional challenges. They provide a structured approach to addressing difficult emotions.

Spiritual Exploration: Prompts and triggers can guide spiritual seekers in exploring deeper questions, experiences, and connections with the divine or the transcendent.

Mindfulness and Meditation: Incorporating prompts and triggers into mindfulness practices can deepen awareness and foster a more profound connection with the present moment.

Problem Solving: When faced with complex problems or decisions, prompts and triggers can help you clarify your thoughts and generate potential solutions.

How to Effectively Use Prompts and Triggers in Automatic Writing

Incorporating prompts and triggers into your automatic writing practice can enhance its depth and efficacy. Here's a step-by-step guide on how to use them effectively:

Choose Your Prompt or Trigger: Start by selecting a prompt or trigger that aligns with your goals or intentions for the writing session. Consider what you want to explore or achieve.

Set the Stage: Create a conducive environment for your writing session. Eliminate distractions, choose a comfortable setting, and have your writing materials ready.

Introduce the Prompt or Trigger: Begin your session by introducing the selected prompt or trigger. If using a written prompt, read it aloud or write it at the top of your page. If using a trigger, evoke the sensory or emotional experience associated with it.

Engage in Stream of Consciousness: Allow your thoughts to flow freely in response to the prompt or trigger. Write without self-censorship, judgment, or concern for structure or grammar. Let your subconscious mind lead the way.

Embrace Spontaneity: Be open to unexpected thoughts, emotions, and associations that arise. Follow the tangents and connections that emerge naturally from your initial response.

Stay Present: Focus on the process of writing and your inner experiences. Pay attention to how the prompt or trigger influences your thoughts and emotions.

Set a Time Limit: Depending on your preferences, you can set a timer for your session. Shorter sessions may last 10-15 minutes, while longer ones can extend to 30 minutes or more.

Reflect and Review: After the session, take time to reflect on what you've written. Consider any insights, patterns, or emotions that emerged in response to the prompt or trigger.

Repeat and Experiment: Experiment with different prompts and triggers to explore various aspects of your inner world. Revisit the same prompts periodically to observe how your responses evolve over time.

Examples of Prompts and Triggers

Prompts and triggers can vary widely in content and style, making them versatile tools for automatic writing. Here are examples of prompts and triggers to inspire your practice:

Prompts

1. Write about a time when you felt completely at peace.
2. Explore your earliest childhood memory in detail.
3. Describe a dream you had recently and its emotional impact.
4. What does success mean to you, and how do you measure it?
5. Write a letter to your future self, reflecting on your hopes and aspirations.

Triggers

1. The scent of rain-soaked earth after a summer storm.

2. The image of a solitary tree against a fiery sunset.

3. The feeling of nostalgia that washes over you when you hear a certain song.

4. The taste of a favorite childhood treat or comfort food.

5. The sensation of warmth and comfort when wrapped in a cozy blanket.

Prompts and triggers are powerful keys that unlock the door to your inner world, igniting a dialogue with your subconscious mind. By incorporating these tools into your automatic writing practice, you can explore the depths of your creativity, gain insights into your thoughts and emotions, and embark on a journey of self-discovery and self-expression. Whether you use prompts and triggers for personal growth, creative inspiration, or emotional healing, they are versatile companions on your path to unlocking the treasures of your inner landscape. Embrace their guidance, and let your automatic writing practice flourish with newfound depth and meaning.

Guided Writing Exercises

Guided writing exercises are structured and intentional prompts that lead you on a purposeful journey of self-expression, creativity, and self-discovery. Unlike stream of consciousness writing, which flows freely without constraints, guided exercises provide a clear roadmap for your writing session. They offer a structured framework that can be tailored to specific goals, whether you seek to enhance your creative skills, explore your inner world, or achieve personal growth. In this exploration, we will delve into the significance of guided writing exercises, explore their diverse applications, and provide guidance on how to effectively incorporate them into your practice.

The Essence of Guided Writing Exercises

Guided writing exercises are designed to encourage a focused and intentional exploration of specific themes, emotions, or concepts. They offer a set of instructions or prompts that steer your writing in a particular direction, allowing you to delve deep into chosen aspects of your inner world. While they provide structure, guided exercises still leave ample room for your unique perspective and creative expression.

Here's a breakdown of key elements:

Structure: Guided writing exercises provide a clear structure and set of instructions to follow during your writing session. They may include specific questions, prompts, or guidelines to direct your thoughts and words.

Purpose: Each exercise is designed with a specific purpose or goal in mind. This purpose can range from stimulating creativity and problem-solving to exploring emotions, memories, or personal values.

Focus: Guided exercises encourage you to focus your attention on the chosen theme or concept. They help you explore it in depth, fostering a richer understanding and insight.

The Significance of Guided Writing Exercises

Guided writing exercises offer several key advantages for writers and practitioners:

Clarity of Intention: They provide a clear intention and focus for your writing session, helping you channel your thoughts and creativity in a purposeful direction.

Enhanced Creativity: Guided exercises stimulate creativity by encouraging fresh perspectives and unique responses to specific themes or prompts.

Structured Exploration: They offer a structured approach to exploring complex emotions, memories, or personal growth topics, making the process more accessible and manageable.

Self-Reflection: Guided exercises promote self-reflection and introspection, allowing you to gain insights into your thoughts, feelings, and beliefs.

Problem Solving: They can be used as problem-solving tools, helping you analyze challenges, generate solutions, and develop action plans.

Personal Growth: Guided writing exercises are valuable tools for personal growth, enabling you to set intentions, clarify goals, and work through issues or unresolved emotions.

Applications of Guided Writing Exercises

Guided writing exercises are versatile tools that can be applied to a wide range of purposes and objectives:

Creative Writing: Writers often use guided exercises to generate ideas, develop characters, or explore plot twists. These exercises can serve as prompts for fiction or poetry.

Journaling: Guided exercises are effective for journaling, offering structured prompts to explore personal experiences, goals, or daily reflections.

Personal Development: Practitioners use guided writing exercises for personal growth, addressing topics like self-esteem, gratitude, forgiveness, or life purpose.

Emotional Healing: Guided exercises can aid in processing and healing emotional wounds, trauma, or grief by providing a structured outlet for expression.

Mindfulness and Meditation: Incorporating guided exercises into mindfulness practices can deepen awareness and promote a more profound connection with the present moment.

Therapeutic Writing: Mental health professionals often integrate guided writing exercises into therapy to help clients explore emotions, work through challenges, and achieve therapeutic goals.

How to Effectively Use Guided Writing Exercises

Incorporating guided writing exercises into your practice requires a deliberate and thoughtful approach. Here's a step-by-step guide on how to use them effectively:

Select a Guided Exercise: Choose a guided writing exercise that aligns with your goals or intentions for the writing session. Consider what you want to explore or achieve.

Create a Conducive Environment: Prepare your writing space, eliminating distractions and ensuring you have the necessary materials at hand.

Introduce the Exercise: Start your session by introducing the guided exercise. If using written prompts, read them aloud or write them at the top of your page. If using digital prompts, have them readily accessible.

Follow Instructions: Carefully follow the instructions provided in the guided exercise. Pay attention to any specific questions or prompts and use them as a starting point for your writing.

Engage in Reflective Writing: Write in response to the exercise, reflecting on the theme or concept presented. Allow your thoughts and feelings to flow naturally as you explore the chosen topic.

Stay on Track: Keep your writing focused on the exercise's theme or intention. While spontaneous insights are welcome, try to maintain a connection with the exercise's guidance.

Set a Time Limit: Depending on your preferences, you can set a timer for your session. Shorter sessions may last 10-15 minutes, while longer ones can extend to 30 minutes or more.

Reflect and Review: After completing the guided exercise, take time to review what you've written. Consider any insights, emotions, or revelations that emerged during the session.

Repeat and Experiment: Experiment with different guided exercises to explore various aspects of your inner world. Revisit exercises periodically to observe how your responses evolve over time.

Examples of Guided Writing Exercises

Guided writing exercises can vary widely in content and purpose, catering to diverse goals and intentions. Here are examples of guided exercises to inspire your practice:

Gratitude Journaling: Write about three things you're grateful for today and why they hold significance for you.

Character Development: Describe a fictional character's daily routine, personality traits, and inner thoughts.

Problem-Solving Exercise: Identify a current challenge you're facing and brainstorm possible solutions and action steps.

Emotional Inventory: Reflect on a recent emotional experience, describing the emotions you felt and the situations or triggers that led to them.

Life Vision Statement: Write a statement that describes your ideal life, incorporating elements like career, relationships, health, and personal growth.

Stream of Consciousness with a Theme: Engage in stream of consciousness writing with a specific theme in mind, such as "freedom," "forgiveness," or "adventure."

Guided writing exercises are like compasses that guide you through the intricate terrain of your inner world. They offer structure, intention, and purpose, enhancing your practice of automatic writing and self-expression. By incorporating guided exercises into your writing routine, you can tap into your creativity, gain deeper insights into your thoughts and emotions, and embark on a meaningful journey of self-discovery and personal growth. Embrace the guidance of these exercises, and let your writing flourish with purpose, depth, and clarity.

Meditation and Mindfulness: Cultivating Inner Presence and Tranquility

Meditation and mindfulness are powerful practices that foster inner presence, emotional well-being, and mental clarity. Rooted in ancient traditions, these practices have found a place in contemporary life as effective tools for managing stress, enhancing focus, and nurturing a deeper connection with oneself. In this exploration, we will delve into the significance of meditation and mindfulness, their diverse applications, and practical guidance on how to incorporate them into your daily routine.

Understanding Meditation and Mindfulness

Meditation is a structured practice that involves focused attention and mental discipline. It encompasses a variety of techniques and traditions, all aimed at quieting the mind, cultivating inner awareness, and accessing a state of profound calm. Meditation practices can include mindfulness meditation, loving-kindness meditation, Zen meditation, and many others. While the specific techniques may differ, the essence remains the same: directing attention inward to observe and transcend the chatter of the mind.

Mindfulness, on the other hand, is a mental state cultivated through the practice of meditation and extended to daily life. It involves purposeful and non-judgmental awareness of the present moment. Mindfulness encourages observing thoughts, emotions, and sensations without attachment or aversion. This state of heightened awareness allows individuals to respond to life's challenges with greater equanimity and clarity.

The Significance of Meditation and Mindfulness

Meditation and mindfulness hold profound significance in the realm of personal growth, mental health, and well-being:

Stress Reduction: Both practices have been shown to reduce stress levels by promoting relaxation and fostering resilience in the face of life's challenges.

Emotional Regulation: Meditation and mindfulness can enhance emotional intelligence and promote healthier responses to emotions, reducing impulsivity and reactivity.

Mental Clarity: These practices sharpen focus and improve cognitive function, making it easier to concentrate on tasks and make informed decisions.

Enhanced Well-Being: Regular meditation and mindfulness are associated with increased life satisfaction, happiness, and a greater sense of inner peace.

Self-Awareness: These practices encourage self-reflection and self-awareness, helping individuals gain insight into their thoughts, beliefs, and behavioral patterns.

Mind-Body Connection: Meditation and mindfulness recognize the profound connection between the mind and body, promoting overall physical and mental health.

Spiritual Growth: For many, meditation is a path to spiritual growth and enlightenment, fostering a deeper connection with the self and the universe.

Applications of Meditation and Mindfulness

Meditation and mindfulness are versatile practices with applications in various aspects of life:

Stress Management: Meditation and mindfulness techniques are effective tools for managing stress, anxiety, and overwhelm. By cultivating inner calm, they help individuals navigate challenging situations with greater ease.

Emotional Well-Being: These practices promote emotional regulation, reduce symptoms of depression, and enhance overall mental health. They provide a framework for processing and understanding emotions.

Relationships: Mindfulness can improve relationships by fostering empathy, active listening, and effective communication. It encourages presence in interactions with others.

Productivity and Focus: Meditation enhances focus and concentration, improving productivity and performance in work and daily tasks.

Physical Health: Meditation has been linked to improved physical health, including lower blood pressure, reduced inflammation, and enhanced immune function.

Creativity: Mindfulness practices can unlock creativity by quieting the mind and allowing space for new ideas to emerge.

Spiritual Exploration: For those on a spiritual journey, meditation can be a profound tool for self-discovery, insight, and connecting with higher consciousness.

Practical Guidance for Incorporating Meditation and Mindfulness

Incorporating meditation and mindfulness into your daily routine can be a transformative journey. Here are practical steps to get started and make these practices a meaningful part of your life:

Choose Your Approach: Explore different meditation and mindfulness techniques to find the one that resonates with you. Common approaches include mindfulness meditation, loving-kindness meditation, breath awareness, and guided visualization.

Create a Sacred Space: Dedicate a quiet and comfortable space where you can practice meditation and mindfulness without distractions. It could be a corner of a room, a cozy chair, or a cushion in a peaceful area.

Set Aside Time: Schedule regular practice sessions, even if they're brief. Consistency is key to experiencing the benefits. Start with just a few minutes each day and gradually increase the duration as you become more comfortable.

Begin with Mindfulness: Mindfulness can be incorporated into daily activities. Practice being fully present during routine tasks like eating, walking, or washing dishes. Observe the sensations, thoughts, and emotions that arise without judgment.

Embrace Guided Practices: Utilize guided meditation and mindfulness apps or resources. These can provide structured sessions and instructions, making it easier for beginners to start.

Focus on Breath: Many meditation practices center around the breath. Pay attention to the natural rhythm of your breath as you inhale and exhale. This anchors your awareness in the present moment.

Observe Your Thoughts: During meditation, you'll likely encounter thoughts. Instead of resisting them, observe them impartially. Let them pass like clouds in the sky, without attachment or judgment.

Practice Loving-Kindness: Loving-kindness meditation involves sending goodwill and positive intentions to yourself and others. It can promote feelings of compassion and connection.

Seek Guidance: If you're new to meditation or mindfulness, consider seeking guidance from a teacher or attending group sessions. Expert instruction can deepen your practice.

Be Patient and Kind: Meditation and mindfulness are skills that develop over time. Be patient with yourself and approach your practice with self-compassion, accepting whatever arises during your sessions.

Meditation and mindfulness are transformative practices that invite you on a journey within yourself. By cultivating inner presence, emotional resilience, and mental clarity, these practices empower you to navigate life's challenges with grace and authenticity. Whether you seek stress relief, personal growth, enhanced well-being, or spiritual exploration, meditation and mindfulness offer a path to deeper self-discovery and inner tranquility. Embrace the journey within, and let the transformative power of these practices enrich your life in profound ways.

Chapter 4
Overcoming Writer's Block

In this chapter, we will explore effective strategies and techniques to conquer the common and frustrating phenomenon known as writer's block. Whether you're a seasoned writer or just starting out, you'll discover practical methods to rekindle your creativity, regain your writing flow, and overcome the barriers that stand in the way of your writing goals.

Identifying and Addressing Writer's Blocks

Writer's block, the bane of every writer's existence, can strike at the most inconvenient times and leave you feeling creatively stranded. Whether you're working on a novel, an essay, or any form of writing, facing a block can be frustrating. However, it's essential to understand that writer's block is a common challenge, and there are effective ways to identify and address it. In this exploration, we'll delve into the various forms of writer's block, their underlying causes, and practical strategies to overcome them, so you can unleash your creative potential.

Understanding Writer's Block

Writer's block is a broad term that encompasses a range of obstacles that hinder the writing process. These obstacles can manifest in various ways, each with its unique characteristics and triggers. Some common forms of writer's block include:

Blank Page Syndrome: You stare at a blank page, unable to get started or put your thoughts into words.

Perfectionism: You constantly edit and revise your work as you write, striving for perfection in each sentence, which leads to slow progress.

Self-Doubt: You doubt your abilities as a writer, constantly questioning whether your writing is good enough.

Lack of Inspiration: You struggle to find inspiration or ideas for your writing, feeling as though your creative well has run dry.

Overwhelm: You feel overwhelmed by the scale of your writing project, causing you to procrastinate or avoid it altogether.

Fear of Failure: You're afraid that your writing won't meet your own or others' expectations, leading to avoidance.

Comparing Yourself to Others: You constantly compare your work to that of other writers, feeling inadequate or discouraged by their success.

Each form of writer's block has its unique triggers, but they often share common underlying causes, such as anxiety, self-criticism, and excessive pressure to perform.

Identifying the Causes

To effectively address writer's block, it's crucial to identify the specific causes that are impeding your creative flow. Here are some common underlying causes:

Perfectionism: The desire to write flawlessly can lead to excessive self-criticism and editing, slowing down your progress.

Self-Doubt: Insecurity about your writing skills or the value of your ideas can undermine your confidence and motivation.

Lack of Preparation: Insufficient research or planning can make you feel directionless, contributing to a block.

Burnout: Overworking or neglecting self-care can drain your creative energy, leading to a mental block.

External Pressure: Deadlines, expectations from others, or the need to impress can create anxiety and hinder your creative process.

Comparisons: Constantly comparing your work to others can undermine your confidence and stifle your unique voice.

Strategies to Address Writer's Blocks

Now that we've identified the forms and potential causes of writer's block, let's explore effective strategies to overcome these obstacles and reignite your creative flow:

Freewriting: Embrace the practice of freewriting, where you write without self-censorship or concern for perfection. Let your thoughts flow freely, even if they seem disjointed. This helps break through the initial resistance of a blank page.

Set Realistic Goals: Break your writing project into manageable tasks and set achievable goals. This reduces the feeling of overwhelm and creates a sense of progress.

Change Your Environment: Sometimes, a change of scenery can stimulate creativity. Try writing in a different location or under different conditions to see if it helps.

Create a Writing Routine: Establish a consistent writing routine. Set aside dedicated time each day for writing, whether you feel inspired or not. The routine helps condition your mind to be ready for creative work.

Practice Mindfulness: Mindfulness techniques can help alleviate anxiety and self-doubt. Focus on the present moment and observe your thoughts without judgment.

Write Badly on Purpose: Give yourself permission to write poorly in your initial drafts. The goal is to get words on paper; you can always revise and improve later.

Eliminate Distractions: Identify and eliminate distractions in your writing environment. Turn off notifications, close unnecessary tabs on your computer, and create a focused workspace.

Take Breaks: Avoid burnout by taking regular breaks during your writing sessions. Short, frequent breaks can refresh your mind and prevent mental fatigue.

Seek Inspiration: Engage in activities that inspire you, whether it's reading, listening to music, or exploring nature. Inspiration often strikes when you least expect it.

Cultivate Self-Compassion: Replace self-criticism with self-compassion. Understand that writer's block is a common challenge and doesn't define your worth as a writer.

Set Aside Perfection: Release the need for perfection in your first draft. Accept that writing is a process of revision and improvement.

Use Writing Prompts: Writing prompts can provide a starting point and spark your creativity. They bypass the intimidation of a blank page.

Connect with Supportive Writers: Join writing groups, forums, or communities where you can connect with fellow writers who understand the challenges you're facing. Sharing experiences and seeking advice can be motivating.

Practice Visualization: Before you start writing, visualize yourself in a creative flow, fully engaged in your work. This mental preparation can help remove mental blocks.

Take Notes: Keep a notebook or digital document for jotting down ideas, fragments, or inspirations as they come to you throughout the day.

Experiment with Different Genres: If you're stuck in one genre or style, try writing in a different genre or style to stimulate your creativity.

Set Realistic Expectations: Manage external pressure and expectations by setting realistic goals and communicating your needs with others.

Professional Help: If writer's block persists and significantly impacts your well-being, consider seeking guidance from a therapist or counselor who specializes in creative challenges.

Writer's block may be an inevitable part of the creative process, but it doesn't have to be an insurmountable obstacle. By identifying its forms and causes and applying practical strategies, you can navigate through the challenges, reignite your creative spark, and continue your journey as a writer. Remember that writer's block is a common experience shared by many writers, and with patience, self-compassion, and persistence, you can overcome it and unlock your creative potential.

Using Automatic Writing to Break Through Writer's Block

Writer's block, a formidable adversary for every writer, can at times feel insurmountable. When the words refuse to flow and creativity feels stifled, it's natural to seek unconventional methods to break through the blockage. One such method that has proven effective for many writers is automatic writing. In this exploration, we'll delve into how automatic writing can be a powerful tool to overcome writer's block and reignite your creative spark.

Understanding Automatic Writing

Automatic writing, also known as "free writing" or "stream of consciousness writing," is a practice that involves writing without conscious thought or self-censorship. Instead of carefully crafting sentences and paragraphs, you allow your thoughts to flow freely onto the page. This unfiltered stream of words can reveal insights, ideas, and emotions that lie beneath the surface of your conscious mind.

The process of automatic writing typically involves the following steps:

Preparation: Set aside a dedicated time and space for your writing session. Eliminate distractions and create a focused environment.

Setting Intentions: Before you begin, set an intention or question in your mind. This can be a specific writing goal or a general desire to break through writer's block.

Writing Freely: Start writing without a predetermined structure or topic. Let your thoughts flow naturally, even if they seem disorganized or unrelated.

No Self-Censorship: Avoid editing or censoring your thoughts. The goal is to bypass your inner critic and allow your subconscious mind to express itself.

Flow of Words: Write continuously for a set period, whether it's 10 minutes or longer. Keep your pen moving or your fingers typing, even if you're unsure of what to write next.

Reflection: After your session, take time to review what you've written. Look for any interesting ideas, insights, or themes that may have emerged.

Breaking Through Writer's Block with Automatic Writing

Now, let's explore how automatic writing can be a valuable tool for overcoming writer's block:

Bypassing Perfectionism: Writer's block often stems from the desire to write perfectly from the start. Automatic writing frees you from this constraint, as it encourages a raw and unedited expression of your thoughts. By accepting imperfection, you remove a significant barrier to writing.

Accessing the Subconscious: Automatic writing taps into your subconscious mind, where creativity often resides. By allowing your thoughts to flow freely, you can uncover hidden ideas, perspectives, and solutions that may be elusive when writing consciously.

Silencing the Inner Critic: The inner critic, that nagging voice of self-doubt, can be a major contributor to writer's block. Automatic writing drowns out this critic by focusing on the act of writing itself, not the quality of the writing. This can create a sense of freedom and creative liberation.

Generating Ideas: If you're stuck for ideas or inspiration, automatic writing can serve as a brainstorming tool. By writing without a specific topic in mind, you may stumble upon intriguing concepts or themes that spark your creativity.

Overcoming Perfectionism: Perfectionism is a common cause of writer's block. When you write automatically, you become more comfortable with imperfection and are more likely to embrace the messy, creative process.

Unblocking Emotions: Sometimes, emotional blocks can hinder your writing. Automatic writing can help you explore and release these emotions, allowing you to write more freely.

Getting Unstuck: When you're stuck in a particular scene, chapter, or plot point, automatic writing can provide an opportunity to explore alternative directions or solutions. It can help you move forward when you're feeling stuck.

Finding Your Voice: Automatic writing can be a powerful tool for discovering and refining your unique writing voice. By allowing your true thoughts and feelings to surface, you can connect with your authentic style.

Tips for Effective Automatic Writing

To make the most of automatic writing as a tool to break through writer's block, consider the following tips:

Set an Intention: Before each session, set a clear intention or question. This can help guide your subconscious mind and focus your writing.

Create a Ritual: Establish a ritual or routine for your automatic writing sessions. This can signal to your mind that it's time to shift into a creative mode.

No Judgments: Remember that there are no right or wrong answers in automatic writing. Release any judgments about the quality of your writing during the process.

Stay Consistent: Regular practice can enhance the effectiveness of automatic writing. Try to incorporate it into your daily or weekly routine.

Embrace Uncertainty: It's okay not to know where your writing is headed. Embrace the uncertainty, and trust that insights will emerge as you write.

Review and Reflect: After each session, take time to review what you've written. Look for patterns, themes, or ideas that stand out.

Combine with Other Techniques: Automatic writing can complement other creative practices, such as journaling, brainstorming, or meditation. Experiment with combining these techniques to enhance your creative flow.

Automatic writing is a potent gateway to creative liberation. By bypassing self-censorship, silencing your inner critic, and accessing the depths of your subconscious mind, you can break through writer's block and rediscover your creative flow. It's a practice that celebrates imperfection, embraces uncertainty, and fosters the raw, unfiltered expression of your thoughts and ideas. So, the next time you find yourself facing writer's block, consider turning to automatic writing as a trusted companion on your creative journey.

Building Consistency in Your Writing Practice

Consistency in your writing practice is the foundation upon which creativity flourishes and skills sharpen. It's the steady drumbeat that propels your projects forward and transforms aspirations into achievements. Whether you're an aspiring author, a seasoned writer, or someone seeking to infuse more writing into your life, cultivating consistency is essential. In this exploration, we'll delve into the significance of consistency in your writing journey and offer practical guidance on how to build and maintain it.

The Power of Consistency in Writing

Consistency is a potent force in the realm of writing, offering a multitude of benefits:

Skill Development: Consistent writing hones your craft and sharpens your skills. The more you write, the better you become at expressing ideas, crafting narratives, and engaging readers.

Creative Flow: Regular writing sessions establish a rhythm that enhances your creative flow. The more you immerse yourself in the writing process, the more readily ideas and inspiration flow.

Productivity: Consistency breeds productivity. It ensures that you make steady progress on your projects, whether you're writing a novel, blog, or personal journal.

Overcoming Writer's Block: Consistent writing diminishes the impact of writer's block. When writing is a regular habit, you're less likely to be deterred by the occasional creative slump.

Achieving Goals: Whether your goal is to complete a manuscript, publish articles regularly, or simply write more in your daily life, consistency is the key to turning those goals into reality.

Confidence Building: Meeting your writing goals consistently boosts your confidence as a writer. It reinforces the belief that you can accomplish what you set out to do.

Practical Strategies for Building Consistency

Building and maintaining consistency in your writing practice requires intentional effort and a strategic approach. Here are practical strategies to help you establish a consistent writing routine:

Set Clear Goals: Define your writing goals and be specific. Are you aiming to write a certain number of words per day, complete a manuscript by a certain date, or publish weekly blog posts? Clarity about your objectives is crucial.

Create a Writing Schedule: Set aside dedicated time for writing in your daily or weekly schedule. Treat this time as non-negotiable, just like any other appointment.

Start Small: If you're new to writing consistently, begin with manageable goals. It's better to write a few hundred words consistently than to set an ambitious target that becomes overwhelming.

Establish Rituals: Create rituals or routines around your writing time to signal to your mind that it's time to shift into creative mode. This could involve making a cup of tea, lighting a candle, or listening to specific music.

Use Writing Prompts: When you're unsure of what to write, use writing prompts to jumpstart your creativity. Prompts provide a starting point and can help you bypass initial resistance.

Accountability Partners: Partner with a writing buddy or join a writing group to hold each other accountable. Sharing your progress and challenges with others can provide motivation.

Track Your Progress: Keep a writing journal or use digital tools to track your progress. Record your word count, the time spent writing, and any insights or breakthroughs.

Embrace Flexibility: While consistency is vital, be flexible in your approach. Life may throw curveballs, and it's okay to adjust your writing schedule when necessary.

Set Rewards: Reward yourself for meeting your writing goals. Treat yourself to something you enjoy, whether it's a special meal, a favorite book, or a leisurely walk.

Eliminate Distractions: Create a distraction-free writing environment. Turn off notifications, close unnecessary tabs on your computer, and find a quiet space where you can focus.

Mindful Writing: Approach your writing practice with mindfulness. Be present in the moment, fully engaged with your words and ideas. Mindfulness can enhance the quality of your writing.

Celebrate Milestones: Celebrate your writing milestones, whether it's completing a chapter, hitting a word count goal, or publishing an article. Acknowledging your achievements keeps motivation high.

Join Writing Challenges: Participate in writing challenges or events, such as National Novel Writing Month (NaNoWriMo) or writing marathons. These events provide a supportive community and structured goals.

Learn to Say No: Guard your writing time by learning to say no to activities or commitments that could encroach on it. Prioritize your writing as a valuable part of your life.

Morning Pages: Consider adopting the practice of morning pages, where you write stream-of-consciousness for a few pages each morning. This practice can clear your mind and spark creativity.

Batching Tasks: If you have multiple writing projects, consider batching similar tasks together. For example, dedicate certain days to drafting, others to editing, and others to research.

Stay Inspired: Continuously seek inspiration from books, art, nature, and life experiences. Inspiration fuels your creativity and motivates you to write consistently.

Review and Reflect: Periodically review your writing goals and progress. Reflect on what's working and what could be improved in your consistency-building efforts.

Overcoming Challenges and Maintaining Consistency

Building consistency in your writing practice may not always be smooth sailing. Challenges like writer's block, external demands, and self-doubt may arise. To maintain consistency in the face of these challenges:

Accept Imperfection: Understand that not every writing session will yield perfect results. Embrace imperfection and focus on the process, not just the outcome.

Revisit Your Goals: When facing challenges, revisit your writing goals to remind yourself of your motivation and purpose. Sometimes, this can reignite your determination.

Practice Self-Compassion: Be kind and patient with yourself. Don't berate yourself for missed writing sessions or perceived failures. Treat yourself with the same compassion you would offer a friend.

Adapt and Adjust: If your initial strategy isn't working, be willing to adapt and adjust your approach. Experiment with different routines, tools, or techniques to find what works best for you.

Seek Support: Reach out to your writing community or support system when facing challenges. They can provide encouragement, advice, and a listening ear.

Consistency in your writing practice is a journey, not a destination. It's a commitment to your creativity and a testament to your dedication as a writer. By setting clear goals, establishing routines, and embracing flexibility, you can build and maintain consistency in your writing practice. Remember that the path to creative mastery is paved with the words you write consistently, one day at a time.

Chapter 5
Exploring Creativity Through Automatic Writing

In this chapter, we'll embark on a journey of creative exploration through the practice of automatic writing. Discover how this liberating process can unearth hidden depths of your imagination, foster innovation, and open doors to uncharted creative territories.

Connecting with Your Inner Creativity

Creativity, often considered a wellspring of innovation, inspiration, and personal expression, is a force that resides within each of us. It's not limited to artists, writers, or musicians; it's a fundamental aspect of human nature waiting to be tapped into and harnessed. In this exploration, we'll delve into the depths of creativity, uncover its significance, and offer practical insights and exercises to help you connect with your inner creativity and awaken its potential in your life.

Understanding Creativity

Creativity is a multifaceted and elusive concept that defies easy definition. It encompasses the ability to generate novel ideas, think critically, solve problems, and express oneself in unique ways. Creativity can manifest in various forms, from artistic endeavors like painting and writing to scientific breakthroughs, entrepreneurial innovations, and everyday problem-solving.

At its core, creativity involves:

Originality: The capacity to produce ideas, concepts, or solutions that are novel and distinctive.

Flexibility: The willingness to explore diverse perspectives, ideas, and approaches.

Adaptability: The ability to adjust and refine creative endeavors based on feedback and changing circumstances.

Risk-Taking: A willingness to venture beyond the familiar and embrace uncertainty.

Persistence: The commitment to see creative projects through, even in the face of challenges.

Passion: A deep enthusiasm and engagement with the creative process.

The Significance of Creativity

Creativity is not merely a skill; it's a vital aspect of personal and societal growth, development, and well-being:

Problem Solving: Creativity equips individuals with the tools to devise innovative solutions to complex problems, whether in science, business, or personal life.

Self-Expression: It provides a means for individuals to express their thoughts, emotions, and unique perspectives, fostering a sense of identity and fulfillment.

Innovation: Creativity is the driving force behind technological advancements, artistic masterpieces, and groundbreaking discoveries.

Emotional Well-Being: Engaging in creative activities can reduce stress, boost mood, and promote mental health by providing an outlet for self-expression and emotional processing.

Communication: Creativity enhances effective communication by allowing individuals to convey ideas, stories, and messages in engaging and memorable ways.

Personal Growth: Exploring one's creative potential can lead to personal growth, increased self-confidence, and a deeper understanding of oneself.

Collaboration: Creativity fosters collaboration and teamwork, as diverse perspectives and ideas come together to create innovative solutions.

Connecting with Your Inner Creativity

Connecting with your inner creativity is a process of self-discovery and self-expression. It involves recognizing and embracing your creative potential. Here are practical steps to help you connect with your inner creativity:

Embrace Curiosity: Cultivate a curious mindset. Approach the world with wonder and a thirst for knowledge. Ask questions, explore new interests, and seek out novel experiences.

Create Space: Dedicate physical and mental space for creative exploration. Set aside time for creative activities, whether it's writing, painting, or brainstorming ideas.

Silence Self-Doubt: Overcome self-doubt by acknowledging that everyone has creative potential. Don't be deterred by thoughts of inadequacy or comparison to others.

Practice Mindfulness: Mindfulness techniques, such as meditation and deep breathing, can help quiet the mind, reduce anxiety, and create a receptive environment for creativity to flourish.

Keep a Creative Journal: Maintain a journal to capture ideas, thoughts, and inspirations. Use it to explore your inner world and jot down creative sparks.

Engage in Play: Reconnect with the joy of play and experimentation. Engage in activities that stimulate your imagination, whether it's playing with art supplies, building with LEGO bricks, or trying out new hobbies.

Break Routine: Step out of your comfort zone and break routine. Novel experiences and environments can stimulate creativity by challenging established patterns of thinking.

Surround Yourself with Inspiration: Fill your environment with sources of inspiration, such as books, art, music, and nature. These stimuli can trigger creative thoughts and ideas.

Collaborate and Share: Collaborate with others who share your interests or passions. Sharing ideas and perspectives can spark creativity and provide valuable feedback.

Celebrate Mistakes: Embrace the idea that mistakes are part of the creative process. Don't fear failure; instead, view it as an opportunity for growth and learning.

Practical Exercises to Awaken Creativity

To further unlock your inner creativity, engage in these practical exercises:

Free Writing: Set aside a specific time each day for free writing. Write without self-censorship or concern for grammar and punctuation. Let your thoughts flow freely.

Mind Mapping: Use mind maps to visually explore ideas and concepts. Start with a central theme or word and branch out with related ideas and associations.

Creative Prompts: Use creative prompts as a springboard for writing, drawing, or brainstorming. Prompts can provide a starting point when you're feeling stuck.

Visual Journaling: Create a visual journal by combining words and images. Use collage, drawing, and writing to express your thoughts and emotions.

Role Reversal: Explore a situation or problem from different perspectives. Imagine how someone else, whether fictional or real, might approach it.

Random Word Association: Select a random word or phrase and let your mind wander, making associations and connections. This exercise can lead to unexpected ideas.

Five Senses Exploration: Engage your five senses to observe your surroundings in detail. Use descriptive language to capture what you see, hear, touch, taste, and smell.

Storytelling from Objects: Choose an everyday object and create a story or narrative around it. Give it a history, a purpose, and characters.

Reverse Thinking: Start with an unconventional or opposite idea and work backward to explore its implications. This can lead to unique perspectives and solutions.

Creative Writing Prompts: Explore creative writing prompts that encourage imaginative storytelling or evoke emotions.

Overcoming Creative Blocks

It's common to encounter creative blocks along your journey to connect with your inner creativity. When faced with such obstacles, consider these strategies:

Take Breaks: Stepping away from a creative project temporarily can provide clarity and fresh insights when you return.

Change Perspective: Look at your work from a different angle or consider alternative viewpoints.

Embrace Constraints: Limitations can sometimes spark creativity. Embrace constraints as opportunities for innovation.

Learn from Others: Study the work of other creators, artists, or writers who inspire you. Analyze their techniques and use them as a source of inspiration.

Collaborate: Collaborating with others can inject new ideas and perspectives into your creative process.

Seek Feedback: Share your work with trusted friends or mentors and solicit constructive feedback.

Connecting with your inner creativity is a transformative journey of self-discovery and self-expression. It's about embracing curiosity, silencing self-doubt, and nurturing a mindset that welcomes exploration and innovation. By engaging in practical exercises, breaking through creative blocks, and celebrating the creative process, you can awaken and nurture your inner creativity, unlocking a world of possibilities and personal fulfillment. Remember, your creativity is a unique and valuable gift waiting to be shared with the world.

Unleashing Your Imagination

Imagination, often described as the gateway to creativity, is a boundless realm of ideas, possibilities, and visions. It's the engine that drives artistic expression, problem-solving, and innovation. In this exploration, we'll delve deep into the concept of imagination, its significance in our lives, and practical strategies to unleash its power, fostering creativity and personal growth.

Understanding Imagination

Imagination is the mental capacity to form new ideas, images, or concepts that are not directly rooted in current reality. It's the ability to create mental representations of things that don't exist, recall past experiences, or visualize future scenarios. Imagination is not limited to the arts; it plays a crucial role in various aspects of life:

Creative Arts: In painting, writing, music, and other creative endeavors, imagination is the driving force behind the generation of original ideas and the transformation of concepts into tangible expressions.

Problem Solving: Imagination fuels innovation and problem-solving by enabling individuals to envision new solutions, question existing paradigms, and explore uncharted territories.

Innovation: In the realm of science, technology, and business, imagination is at the heart of groundbreaking discoveries, inventions, and entrepreneurial ventures.

Empathy: Imagination allows us to put ourselves in others' shoes, fostering understanding, empathy, and the ability to relate to different perspectives and experiences.

Personal Growth: Imagination plays a pivotal role in personal development by helping individuals envision their goals, aspirations, and the pathways to realizing their potential.

Childhood Development: Imagination is a fundamental part of childhood development, aiding in cognitive growth, creativity, and the development of social and emotional skills.

The Significance of Imagination in Creativity

Imagination and creativity are closely intertwined. Creativity is the process of using imagination to generate new and valuable ideas, whether in the form of artistic creations, scientific innovations, or problem-solving strategies. Imagination is the wellspring from which creativity flows, serving as the source of inspiration, innovation, and originality.

Key aspects of the relationship between imagination and creativity include:

Idea Generation: Imagination provides the raw material for creative idea generation. It allows you to envision possibilities and explore concepts beyond the constraints of reality.

Exploration: Imagination encourages exploration and experimentation, enabling you to consider multiple perspectives and unconventional approaches.

Innovation: Imagination is the driving force behind innovation, as it allows you to envision novel solutions, products, and experiences that depart from the familiar.

Expression: Imagination fuels artistic expression, allowing you to convey thoughts, emotions, and stories in unique and engaging ways.

Problem-Solving: Imagination plays a critical role in problem-solving by helping you envision alternative solutions and anticipate potential outcomes.

Practical Strategies to Unleash Your Imagination

Imagination is a skill that can be nurtured and cultivated over time. Here are practical strategies to help you unleash your imagination and harness its creative potential:

Cultivate Curiosity: Embrace curiosity as a driving force in your life. Ask questions, seek answers, and explore subjects that pique your interest. Curiosity is the spark that ignites the flames of imagination.

Divergent Thinking: Practice divergent thinking, which involves generating multiple ideas or solutions to a problem. Set aside judgment and allow yourself to explore all possibilities, even unconventional ones.

Visualize: Use visualization techniques to create mental images of ideas, concepts, or scenarios. Close your eyes and vividly imagine the details of your imagination. Visualization can enhance creativity.

Read Widely: Read books, articles, and literature from various genres and disciplines. Exposure to diverse ideas and perspectives can stimulate your imagination.

Mindfulness Meditation: Engage in mindfulness meditation to clear your mind of distractions and enhance your ability to focus on imaginative thoughts. Mindfulness can help you tap into your creative reservoir.

Nature Connection: Spend time in nature. The beauty and complexity of the natural world can inspire imaginative thinking and creative ideas.

Creativity Exercises: Engage in creativity exercises and games that challenge your imagination. For example, practice brainstorming sessions, word association games, or storytelling challenges.

Daydreaming: Allow yourself to daydream and let your mind wander freely. Daydreaming can lead to unexpected insights and creative sparks.

Visual Arts: Experiment with visual arts, such as drawing, painting, or sculpting. These activities can help you visualize and manifest your imaginative ideas in a tangible form.

Change Perspectives: Look at familiar objects or situations from different angles or viewpoints. Challenge your assumptions and consider alternative possibilities.

Collaborate: Collaborate with others on creative projects. Sharing ideas and perspectives can inspire imaginative thinking and expand your creative horizons.

Seek Inspiration: Surround yourself with sources of inspiration, whether it's visiting museums, attending concerts, or exploring new places. Inspiration often triggers imaginative thought.

Create Mind Maps: Use mind maps to visually represent ideas and connections. Mind mapping can help you organize and explore the complexities of your imagination.

Imaginative Writing: Practice imaginative writing by crafting stories, poems, or essays that draw from your imagination. Writing allows you to explore and articulate your creative thoughts.

Cross-Disciplinary Learning: Explore disciplines outside your comfort zone. Learning from different fields can introduce novel concepts and approaches to your imagination.

Overcoming Creative Blocks in Imagination

Creativity and imagination may face roadblocks at times. When encountering creative blocks, consider these strategies to reignite your imaginative spark:

Embrace Challenges: View creative blocks as challenges to overcome rather than insurmountable obstacles. Embrace them as opportunities for growth and learning.

Change Your Environment: Shift your physical or mental environment to break the monotony and stimulate fresh ideas.

Explore Different Mediums: Experiment with different creative mediums or forms of expression. Trying something new can rekindle your imaginative fire.

Collaborate: Seek collaboration with others who can provide diverse perspectives and inspire imaginative thinking.

Take Breaks: Step away from your creative project for a while. Often, a break allows your mind to process ideas and return with renewed creativity.

Revisit Past Ideas: Revisit old ideas or projects that once excited you. Sometimes, past work can serve as a source of inspiration for new imaginative endeavors.

Unleashing your imagination is akin to tapping into a limitless reservoir of creative potential. It's a journey of self-discovery, self-expression, and personal growth. By embracing curiosity, practicing divergent thinking, and engaging in activities that nurture your imagination, you can harness its power to fuel creativity and innovation in your life. Imagination is not just a mental exercise; it's your creative superpower waiting to be unleashed, offering a gateway to a world of endless possibilities and artistic expression.

Tapping into Your Subconscious Mind

The human mind is a vast and complex landscape, with conscious thoughts and perceptions representing only a fraction of its capabilities. Beneath the surface lies the subconscious mind, a realm teeming with uncharted potential, creativity, and insight. Tapping into your subconscious mind can be a transformative journey, unlocking hidden treasures of creativity, problem-solving abilities, and self-understanding. In this exploration, we'll delve into the depths of the subconscious mind, understand its significance, and unveil practical strategies to access its boundless resources.

Understanding the Subconscious Mind

The subconscious mind is a part of the mind that operates below the level of conscious awareness. It encompasses thoughts, feelings, memories, and beliefs that are not actively in the forefront of your conscious thoughts but still influence your behavior, decisions, and perceptions. To understand the subconscious mind, it's essential to grasp the following key concepts:

Automatic Processing: The subconscious mind is responsible for many automatic processes that occur without conscious effort, such as regulating bodily functions, habits, and intuitive reactions.

Emotional Storage: Emotions and emotional experiences are often stored in the subconscious mind, influencing how you react to situations, people, and events.

Memory Repository: The subconscious mind stores a vast reservoir of memories, including those you may not consciously recall. These memories can shape your preferences, fears, and tendencies.

Belief Systems: Core beliefs and self-perceptions are often deeply rooted in the subconscious. These beliefs can impact self-esteem, confidence, and overall well-being.

Creativity and Problem Solving: The subconscious mind is a fertile ground for creative insights and problem-solving. It can generate ideas, connections, and solutions that the conscious mind may overlook.

Intuition and Gut Feelings: Gut feelings, hunches, and intuition often originate from the subconscious mind's processing of subtle cues and information.

Dreams: Dreams are a manifestation of subconscious processes and can provide valuable insights, symbolism, and messages.

The Significance of the Subconscious Mind

The subconscious mind wields profound influence over your thoughts, emotions, behaviors, and decisions. Its significance extends to various aspects of life:

Creativity: The subconscious mind is a wellspring of creativity, where novel ideas, concepts, and artistic inspiration often originate. It can offer fresh perspectives and innovative solutions.

Problem Solving: When faced with complex problems, the subconscious mind can work tirelessly in the background, sifting through information and generating insights. Many famous inventors and scientists have credited their breakthroughs to insights that surfaced from their subconscious.

Emotional Processing: Emotions, including those deeply buried in the subconscious, shape your emotional responses, relationships, and overall well-being. Exploring and understanding these emotions can lead to emotional healing and growth.

Self-Image: Self-esteem, self-confidence, and self-worth are closely tied to subconscious beliefs and perceptions. Addressing and reshaping these beliefs can lead to positive self-transformation.

Intuition: Trusting your intuition often means tapping into your subconscious mind's ability to process subtle information and provide guidance.

Practical Strategies to Tap into Your Subconscious Mind

Accessing your subconscious mind requires deliberate effort and practice. Here are practical strategies to help you tap into its depths:

Meditation: Regular meditation practice can quiet the conscious mind and create a receptive space for subconscious insights to emerge. Meditation also enhances mindfulness, helping you become more attuned to your thoughts and feelings.

Mindfulness: Incorporate mindfulness into your daily life by paying close attention to your thoughts, emotions, and sensations. Mindfulness can reveal patterns and beliefs hidden in the subconscious.

Journaling: Keep a journal to record your thoughts, dreams, and reflections. Writing can help bring subconscious thoughts to the surface and provide clarity on your emotions and beliefs.

Visualization: Use visualization techniques to actively engage with your subconscious. Create mental images of your goals, desires, and challenges, allowing your subconscious to work on them in the background.

Hypnosis and Self-Hypnosis: Hypnotherapy or self-hypnosis can help you access the subconscious mind through guided relaxation and suggestion. This can be especially effective for addressing specific issues or behaviors.

Creative Expression: Engage in creative activities such as writing, drawing, or music. These outlets can access your subconscious and provide a channel for self-expression.

Dream Analysis: Pay attention to your dreams and keep a dream journal. Analyzing dreams can offer insights into your subconscious thoughts, emotions, and concerns.

Positive Affirmations: Use positive affirmations to reprogram negative or limiting beliefs held in the subconscious. Repeated affirmations can help instill empowering beliefs.

Silence and Solitude: Spend time in silence and solitude to disconnect from external distractions. This allows your subconscious to communicate more clearly with your conscious mind.

Binaural Beats and Brainwave Entrainment: Some people find that listening to binaural beats or brainwave entrainment audio can alter their brainwave patterns, potentially facilitating access to the subconscious.

Creative Problem-Solving: When faced with a challenging problem, take a break from active thinking and allow your subconscious to work on it. Return to the problem later with a refreshed perspective.

Overcoming Blocks and Resistance

Tapping into your subconscious mind may encounter resistance or blocks. Here are strategies to address common challenges:

Patience and Persistence: Subconscious exploration may not yield immediate results. Be patient and persistent in your efforts, and trust that insights will surface over time.

Self-Compassion: Be gentle with yourself during the process. Avoid self-criticism or frustration if progress seems slow or if you encounter resistance.

Emotional Blocks: If you encounter strong emotional resistance, consider seeking support from a therapist or counselor who specializes in working with the subconscious mind.

Fear of the Unknown: Fear or discomfort with what you may uncover in your subconscious is natural. Approach exploration with an open mind and a commitment to self-discovery.

Tapping into your subconscious mind is a profound journey of self-discovery and personal growth. It's a process that can lead to enhanced creativity, problem-solving abilities, emotional healing, and a deeper understanding of yourself. By practicing mindfulness, journaling, visualization, and other techniques, you can unlock the vast potential of your subconscious, ushering in a world of creativity, insight, and personal transformation. Remember that your subconscious mind is a wellspring of wisdom and creativity waiting to be explored and harnessed for your benefit and personal growth.

Chapter 6
Practical Applications

In this chapter, we'll explore the real-world applications of the knowledge and skills you've gained throughout the book. From enhancing your creativity to solving everyday challenges, you'll discover how to put your newfound insights into action and make a meaningful impact on your personal and professional life.

Journaling and Self-Reflection

Journaling is a powerful tool that has been used for centuries to capture thoughts, emotions, and experiences on paper. It serves as a canvas for self-expression, self-discovery, and self-improvement. Through the act of journaling, individuals can gain insights, process emotions, set goals, and track their personal growth journey. In this exploration, we'll delve into the art of journaling, its myriad benefits, and practical strategies for incorporating it into your life.

Understanding Journaling

Journaling involves the practice of writing down your thoughts, feelings, experiences, and observations in a dedicated journal or notebook. It's a form of expressive writing that offers a safe and private space to explore your inner world. Journaling can take various forms, including:

Diary Entries: Daily accounts of your experiences, activities, and emotions.

Reflective Writing: Deep exploration of your thoughts, beliefs, and values.

Creative Writing: Poetry, stories, or creative pieces that reflect your inner world.

Goal Setting: Setting and tracking personal or professional goals.

Gratitude Journaling: Recording things you're thankful for to cultivate positivity.

Stream-of-Consciousness Writing: Unfiltered and spontaneous writing to free your mind.

The Significance of Journaling

Journaling is more than a simple writing exercise; it holds profound significance in personal development and well-being:

Self-Reflection: Journaling prompts self-reflection, helping you gain clarity about your thoughts, feelings, and experiences.

Emotional Processing: It provides an outlet for processing complex emotions, reducing stress, and promoting emotional well-being.

Problem Solving: Journaling can be a tool for problem-solving, helping you explore solutions and weigh pros and cons.

Goal Achievement: By setting and tracking goals in your journal, you can increase your chances of achieving them.

Creativity: Journaling nurtures creativity by allowing you to explore imaginative ideas and free your creative spirit.

Mindfulness: It fosters mindfulness by encouraging you to stay present and engage with your thoughts and experiences.

Self-Discovery: Journaling facilitates self-discovery by uncovering patterns, values, and beliefs that shape your life.

Practical Strategies for Effective Journaling

To reap the benefits of journaling, consider these practical strategies:

Consistency: Establish a regular journaling routine. Whether daily, weekly, or monthly, consistency is key to gaining insights and tracking progress.

Choose Your Medium: Select a journaling medium that suits you. It can be a physical notebook, a digital app, or even audio recordings.

Create a Comfortable Space: Find a quiet and comfortable space where you can write without distractions.

Set Intentions: Begin each journaling session with clear intentions. What do you hope to achieve or explore? Setting intentions gives your writing purpose.

Write Freely: Don't censor or edit yourself. Let your thoughts flow freely, even if they seem trivial or disorganized at first.

Date Your Entries: Date your journal entries to track your progress over time and provide context to your reflections.

Embrace Stream of Consciousness: Try stream-of-consciousness writing, where you write whatever comes to mind without structure or judgment.

Use Prompts: Utilize journaling prompts to spark ideas and guide your writing. Prompts can focus on specific themes, emotions, or goals.

Reflect and Review: Periodically review your past entries to gain insights into your growth, patterns, and changes in perspective.

Practice Gratitude: Dedicate a portion of your journal to gratitude. Write down things you're thankful for to cultivate a positive mindset.

Set Goals: Record your goals and aspirations, breaking them down into actionable steps. Journaling can help you stay accountable.

Track Achievements: Celebrate your achievements, no matter how small. Acknowledging your progress boosts motivation.

Explore Emotions: When processing emotions, be honest and compassionate with yourself. Explore the root causes of your feelings.

Problem-Solve: If you're facing challenges, use journaling to brainstorm solutions and evaluate potential outcomes.

Creative Expression: Experiment with creative forms of journaling, such as poetry, art, or collage, to engage your imagination.

Overcoming Common Challenges in Journaling

While journaling can be immensely rewarding, it's not without its challenges. Here's how to overcome some common obstacles:

Lack of Time: Set aside dedicated time for journaling, even if it's just a few minutes a day. Prioritize self-reflection.

Self-Criticism: Remember that your journal is a judgment-free zone. Don't criticize your writing or thoughts. Embrace imperfection.

Writer's Block: If you're stuck, start by writing about your writer's block itself. Often, this opens the door to other thoughts and ideas.

Overthinking: Don't overthink your entries. Trust that your subconscious will guide your writing in meaningful directions.

Inconsistency: If you struggle with consistency, be forgiving and start anew. It's never too late to resume journaling.

Journaling for Specific Purposes

Depending on your goals and needs, you can tailor your journaling practice to specific purposes:

Gratitude Journal: Focus on what you're grateful for each day to foster positivity.

Goal Journal: Track your goals, break them into tasks, and monitor your progress.

Dream Journal: Record your dreams and explore their symbolism and messages.

Emotional Journal: Express and process your emotions, allowing yourself to let go of negative feelings.

Creative Journal: Use your journal for creative endeavors, such as writing stories, poems, or drawing.

Travel Journal: Document your travel experiences, capturing memories and reflections.

Journaling is a versatile and deeply personal practice that can lead to profound self-discovery and personal growth. By regularly engaging in self-reflection, processing emotions, setting goals, and exploring your creativity, you can harness the power of journaling to gain clarity, insight, and a deeper understanding of yourself. Remember that your journal is your path to self-improvement and a canvas for self-expression. It's a safe space for exploration and a trusted companion on your journey toward personal growth and clarity.

Creative writing, particularly in the realm of fiction, is a captivating journey that allows writers to conjure entire universes, breathe life into characters, and share compelling stories. Whether you aspire to write novels, short stories, or simply want to explore your creativity, delving into the world of fiction is an enriching and fulfilling endeavor. In this exploration, we'll dive into the art of creative writing and fiction, uncover its significance, and offer practical insights for aspiring writers.

Understanding Creative Writing and Fiction

Creative writing is a form of self-expression that encompasses various genres and styles, including fiction, poetry, drama, and creative nonfiction. At its core, creative writing is the art of crafting narratives and stories that engage, inspire, and entertain readers. Fiction, a subset of creative writing, focuses on inventing imaginary worlds, characters, and plots.

Key elements of creative writing in fiction include:

Imagination: Fiction writers draw from their imagination to create unique settings, characters, and scenarios.

Character Development: Crafting compelling characters with distinct personalities, motivations, and growth arcs is a fundamental aspect of fiction.

Plot and Structure: Fiction follows a structured narrative arc with a beginning, middle, and end. Plot development is crucial for keeping readers engaged.

Setting: Fictional stories often unfold in imagined or real-world settings, which contribute to the story's atmosphere and context.

Conflict and Resolution: Conflict is central to fiction, driving the plot and character development. Resolution provides closure and emotional satisfaction.

The Significance of Creative Writing and Fiction

Creative writing and fiction offer numerous benefits and significance:

Self-Expression: Creative writing allows authors to express their thoughts, emotions, and perspectives, providing an outlet for personal expression.

Empathy: Writing from various character perspectives fosters empathy and a deeper understanding of diverse experiences and viewpoints.

Storytelling Tradition: Fiction is an essential part of the storytelling tradition, passing down culture, wisdom, and entertainment through generations.

Escapism: Fiction provides an escape from reality, allowing readers to immerse themselves in different worlds and experiences.

Entertainment: Engaging fiction captivates and entertains readers, providing an enjoyable and memorable experience.

Reflection: Fiction can prompt readers to reflect on their own lives, beliefs, and values through the lens of the characters and situations presented.

Practical Strategies for Creative Writing in Fiction

Becoming a skilled fiction writer involves practice, dedication, and a willingness to learn. Here are practical strategies to help you embark on your creative writing journey:

Read Widely: To become a proficient fiction writer, immerse yourself in a variety of genres and authors. Reading expands your literary horizons and exposes you to different writing styles.

Write Regularly: Develop a writing routine that suits your schedule. Consistency is key to honing your craft.

Start Small: If you're new to fiction writing, begin with short stories or flash fiction. These formats allow you to experiment and refine your storytelling skills.

Character Development: Create well-rounded characters by exploring their backstories, motivations, and desires. Readers should connect with and care about your characters.

Plotting: Outline your story's plot and structure, including key plot points and the story's climax. An organized approach can help you avoid plot holes and maintain reader engagement.

Show, Don't Tell: Instead of explicitly stating emotions or character traits, use descriptive language and actions to show them. This draws readers into the story.

Dialogue: Craft authentic dialogue that reveals character personalities and advances the plot. Dialogue should feel natural and purposeful.

Editing and Revision: Writing is rewriting. After completing a draft, revise and edit your work for clarity, coherence, and style.

Feedback: Seek feedback from trusted peers, writing groups, or writing workshops. Constructive criticism can help you identify areas for improvement.

Expand Your Vocabulary: Enhance your writing by expanding your vocabulary. Use precise and evocative language to paint vivid pictures for your readers.

Embrace Rejection: Rejection is part of the writing journey. Don't be discouraged by rejection letters or criticism. Keep submitting and improving your work.

Read About Writing: Explore books and resources on writing and fiction. Learning from experienced authors can provide valuable insights and techniques.

Overcoming Common Writing Challenges

Writers often face challenges during their creative journey. Here's how to tackle some common obstacles:

Writer's Block: If you experience writer's block, take a break, change your writing environment, or try freewriting to spark creativity.

Self-Doubt: Overcoming self-doubt is essential. Remember that even acclaimed authors face moments of uncertainty. Trust your voice and keep writing.

Lack of Inspiration: Seek inspiration from everyday life, books, art, nature, or personal experiences. Inspiration can strike in unexpected places.

Editing Fatigue: Editing can be exhausting. Take breaks between drafts and consider enlisting the help of beta readers or professional editors.

Genres and Exploration

Fiction encompasses a wide array of genres, each offering its unique storytelling conventions and themes. Exploring different genres can broaden your creative horizons:

Science Fiction: Explores futuristic or speculative concepts, often involving advanced technology, space exploration, or alternative realities.

Fantasy: Features magical or supernatural elements, mythical creatures, and imaginary worlds.

Mystery: Centers around solving a mystery or crime, with suspense and intrigue as key elements.

Romance: Focuses on romantic relationships and emotional connections between characters.

Historical Fiction: Set in a specific historical period, with an emphasis on historical accuracy and atmosphere.

Thriller: Thrillers are characterized by tension, suspense, and high stakes, often involving danger or intrigue.

Literary Fiction: Emphasizes character development, prose style, and themes, often exploring complex human experiences.

Horror: Evokes fear, dread, and shock through supernatural or psychological elements.

Creative writing in fiction is a journey of imagination and storytelling that offers infinite possibilities. Whether you aspire to write novels, short stories, or explore different genres, the art of creative writing allows you to craft worlds, characters, and narratives that resonate with readers. Remember that every word you write contributes to your growth as a writer. Embrace the joy of storytelling, stay committed to your craft, and let your creativity flow as you embark on your journey as a fiction writer.

Problem Solving and Decision Making

Problem solving and decision making are fundamental skills that play a pivotal role in both our personal and professional lives. Whether you're facing complex issues at work, making important life choices, or addressing everyday challenges, the ability to effectively solve problems and make informed decisions is a valuable asset. In this exploration, we'll delve into the art of problem solving and decision making, uncover their significance, and provide practical strategies to enhance your problem-solving and decision-making prowess.

Understanding Problem Solving and Decision Making

Problem Solving: Problem solving is the process of identifying, analyzing, and finding effective solutions to overcome obstacles, achieve goals, or address issues. It involves a systematic approach to understanding the root causes of a problem, generating possible solutions, evaluating their pros and cons, and selecting the best course of action.

Decision Making: Decision making is the act of choosing one option or course of action from among several alternatives. It often follows problem solving, as the information and insights gathered during problem solving inform the decision-making process. Effective decision making involves assessing risks, considering consequences, and aligning choices with your goals and values.

The Significance of Problem Solving and Decision Making

Problem solving and decision making are essential skills for several reasons:

Achieving Goals: Problem solving helps you overcome obstacles that stand between you and your goals. Effective decision making ensures you choose actions that align with your objectives.

Enhancing Efficiency: Sound problem-solving skills enable you to identify inefficiencies and streamline processes, resulting in improved productivity.

Conflict Resolution: Problem solving is crucial for resolving conflicts, whether in personal relationships or in a professional setting.

Innovation: Problem solving often leads to innovative solutions, fostering progress and growth in various fields.

Quality Improvement: Decision making plays a role in maintaining or enhancing the quality of products, services, and outcomes.

Stress Reduction: Effective problem solving and decision making can reduce stress by providing clarity and control in challenging situations.

Practical Strategies for Effective Problem Solving and Decision Making

To become a proficient problem solver and decision maker, consider these practical strategies:

Define the Problem or Decision: Clearly articulate the problem you're facing or the decision you need to make. A well-defined problem is easier to solve.

Gather Information: Collect relevant information, data, and facts that pertain to the problem or decision. Ensure you have a comprehensive understanding of the situation.

Generate Alternatives: Brainstorm a range of possible solutions or options. Encourage creativity and explore unconventional ideas.

Evaluate Alternatives: Assess the pros and cons of each alternative. Consider potential risks, benefits, and consequences.

Set Criteria: Establish criteria or benchmarks against which you'll evaluate the alternatives. These criteria should align with your goals and values.

Make a Decision: Select the alternative that best meets your criteria and aligns with your goals. Trust your judgment and be decisive.

Implement the Decision: Put your chosen solution or decision into action. Develop an implementation plan and execute it effectively.

Monitor and Adapt: Continuously assess the outcomes of your decision or solution. If necessary, be open to adjusting your approach based on feedback and new information.

Overcoming Common Challenges in Problem Solving and Decision Making

Challenges are an inherent part of problem solving and decision making. Here's how to address some common obstacles:

Overthinking: Avoid excessive rumination and analysis paralysis. Trust your judgment and be mindful of decision fatigue.

Emotional Bias: Emotions can cloud judgment. Acknowledge your feelings, but strive to make decisions based on rational analysis and facts.

Confirmation Bias: Be aware of seeking information that confirms your preconceived notions. Actively seek out diverse perspectives and information.

Fear of Failure: Don't let the fear of making mistakes paralyze your decision-making process. Mistakes provide valuable learning experiences.

Lack of Information: When faced with insufficient information, make the best decision you can with the information available. Be prepared to adapt as more information becomes available.

Decision-Making Styles

Individuals often have distinct decision-making styles that influence how they approach problems and choices. These styles can be categorized into several common types:

Analytical: Analytical decision makers are detail-oriented and methodical. They rely on data, facts, and careful analysis to make choices.

Intuitive: Intuitive decision makers trust their gut feelings and instincts. They may rely on hunches and intuition to guide their choices.

Directive: Directive decision makers prefer taking control and making decisions quickly. They often provide clear instructions and take charge in group settings.

Conceptual: Conceptual decision makers are creative and open to exploring unconventional ideas and approaches. They enjoy considering long-term implications.

Behavioral: Behavioral decision makers focus on the human aspect of decisions, considering how choices will affect people and relationships.

Group Decision Making

In many settings, decisions are made by groups rather than individuals. Group decision making can be advantageous because it brings together diverse perspectives and expertise. However, it also comes with its challenges:

Groupthink: Groupthink occurs when a desire for consensus and harmony within the group leads to conformity and a failure to critically evaluate alternatives.

Decision-Making Roles: In group settings, individuals often take on specific roles, such as a facilitator, devil's advocate, or information provider, to ensure a well-rounded decision-making process.

Conflict Resolution: Managing conflicts and disagreements within the group is essential for productive decision making. Constructive conflict resolution can lead to better decisions.

Problem solving and decision making are lifelong skills that empower you to navigate the complexities of life with confidence and clarity. By adopting effective strategies, remaining open to learning, and recognizing and addressing common challenges, you can enhance your problem-solving and decision-making abilities. Remember that every choice you make is an opportunity for growth and learning, and the skills you develop in this journey will serve you well in all aspects of your life.

Personal Growth and Healing

Personal growth and healing are transformative processes that empower individuals to evolve, overcome challenges, and ultimately lead more fulfilling lives. This journey involves self-discovery, self-compassion, and intentional efforts to heal emotional wounds, develop inner strength, and unlock one's true potential. In this exploration, we'll delve into the profound significance of personal growth and healing, explore practical strategies for embarking on this transformative path, and discuss how it can positively impact every aspect of your life.

Understanding Personal Growth and Healing

Personal Growth: Personal growth, often referred to as self-improvement or self-development, is the ongoing process of expanding your self-awareness, acquiring new skills, nurturing positive behaviors, and evolving as an individual. It encompasses physical, emotional, intellectual, and spiritual dimensions of your life. Personal growth is driven by a desire to become the best version of yourself and to reach your full potential.

Healing: Healing, in the context of personal growth, refers to the process of addressing emotional, psychological, or spiritual wounds and traumas. It involves recognizing, acknowledging, and working through past pain and negative experiences. Healing enables individuals to move forward with greater resilience, inner peace, and emotional well-being.

The Significance of Personal Growth and Healing

Personal growth and healing are deeply significant for several reasons:

Self-Discovery: They offer an opportunity to explore your authentic self, uncover your values, and identify your passions and purpose.

Resilience: Personal growth and healing build resilience, helping you bounce back from adversity, setbacks, and challenges.

Emotional Well-Being: Healing emotional wounds contributes to emotional well-being, reducing stress, anxiety, and depression.

Positive Relationships: Personal growth enhances your ability to form healthy, positive relationships with others, based on empathy, compassion, and self-awareness.

Fulfillment: As you grow and heal, you gain a sense of fulfillment and contentment in life, driven by alignment with your values and purpose.

Self-Confidence: Personal growth boosts self-esteem and self-confidence, allowing you to tackle new opportunities and challenges with greater self-assuredness.

Practical Strategies for Personal Growth and Healing

Embarking on a journey of personal growth and healing requires intentional effort and commitment. Here are practical strategies to guide you on this transformative path:

Self-Reflection: Dedicate time to self-reflection. Journaling, meditation, or simply quiet contemplation can help you gain insight into your thoughts, feelings, and life experiences.

Set Clear Goals: Identify specific areas of personal growth you want to focus on. Set clear, achievable goals that align with your values and aspirations.

Seek Knowledge: Continuously seek opportunities to learn and grow. Read books, attend workshops, take courses, and engage in activities that expand your horizons.

Practice Self-Compassion: Be gentle with yourself and practice self-compassion. Acknowledge your imperfections and mistakes as opportunities for growth.

Embrace Change: Personal growth often involves stepping out of your comfort zone. Embrace change and be open to new experiences and challenges.

Healthy Habits: Cultivate healthy habits that support your physical and emotional well-being, such as regular exercise, a balanced diet, and sufficient rest.

Build a Support System: Surround yourself with a supportive network of friends, family, or mentors who encourage your personal growth journey.

Therapy and Counseling: Consider therapy or counseling to address past traumas or emotional wounds. Professional support can be instrumental in the healing process.

Mindfulness and Meditation: Practice mindfulness and meditation to enhance self-awareness, manage stress, and develop inner peace.

Forgiveness: Work on forgiving yourself and others for past hurts. Forgiveness is a powerful healing tool that frees you from the weight of resentment.

Gratitude Practice: Cultivate a gratitude practice to focus on the positive aspects of life. Regularly acknowledge and express gratitude for what you have.

Overcoming Common Challenges in Personal Growth and Healing

On the journey of personal growth and healing, individuals often encounter challenges:

Resistance to Change: Overcoming resistance to change can be difficult. Start with small, manageable steps and gradually expand your comfort zone.

Impatience: Personal growth and healing take time. Be patient with yourself and recognize that progress may be gradual.

Fear of Vulnerability: Healing often requires vulnerability, which can be scary. Remember that vulnerability is a sign of strength, not weakness.

Reluctance to Seek Help: Some individuals hesitate to seek professional support. Recognize that asking for help is a courageous step toward healing and growth.

The Role of Personal Growth in Healing

Personal growth and healing are deeply interconnected. Here's how personal growth contributes to the healing process:

Self-Awareness: Personal growth fosters self-awareness, enabling you to identify and address emotional wounds and triggers.

Self-Compassion: As you grow, you develop self-compassion, which is essential for healing. Self-compassion allows you to treat yourself with kindness and understanding during challenging times.

Resilience: Personal growth builds resilience, helping you bounce back from setbacks and challenges, a crucial aspect of healing.

Positive Coping Mechanisms: As you grow, you acquire healthier coping mechanisms that support emotional well-being and healing.

Empathy and Understanding: Personal growth enhances empathy and understanding of both yourself and others, facilitating the healing of relationships and emotional wounds.

The Impact of Personal Growth and Healing

Personal growth and healing have a profound impact on various aspects of your life:

Relationships: They enable you to form deeper, more meaningful connections with others, fostering healthier and more fulfilling relationships.

Career: Personal growth can lead to increased confidence, motivation, and resilience in your career, opening up new opportunities for success.

Well-Being: They contribute to your overall well-being, reducing stress, anxiety, and depression while promoting emotional resilience and contentment.

Purpose: Personal growth often helps individuals discover or clarify their life purpose, leading to a more meaningful and fulfilling existence.

Personal growth and healing are lifelong journeys of self-discovery, empowerment, and transformation. By embracing these processes, you can heal emotional wounds, expand your self-awareness, and reach your full potential. Remember that personal growth is not a destination but a continuous path of self-improvement and self-compassion. As you embark on this journey, be patient with yourself, seek support when needed, and celebrate your progress along the way. Through personal growth and healing, you can cultivate a life that is deeply fulfilling and aligned with your true self.

Chapter 7
Ethical Considerations

This chapter explores the importance of ethical principles in various aspects of life, from personal relationships to professional endeavors. It delves into the significance of integrity, honesty, and moral values, providing guidance on navigating ethical dilemmas and making principled decisions.

Privacy and Personal Boundaries: Nurturing Healthy Relationships and Well-Being

Privacy and personal boundaries are fundamental aspects of human interaction and well-being. They define the limits of what we are comfortable sharing with others and help create a sense of safety, respect, and autonomy in our relationships and daily lives. In this exploration, we'll delve into the significance of privacy and personal boundaries, understand their role in fostering healthy relationships, and explore practical strategies for establishing and maintaining them.

Understanding Privacy and Personal Boundaries

Privacy: Privacy refers to the right and need for individuals to keep certain aspects of their lives, thoughts, feelings, and activities to themselves or selectively share them with others. It encompasses both physical and emotional boundaries that protect personal information, space, and autonomy.

Personal Boundaries: Personal boundaries are the physical, emotional, and psychological limits we establish to protect our well-being and define our comfort zones in interactions with others. These boundaries help determine how close or distant we allow others to be in our lives.

The Significance of Privacy and Personal Boundaries

Privacy and personal boundaries are of paramount importance for several reasons:

Respect: They are essential for respecting individual autonomy, choices, and personal space. Respecting someone's boundaries is a sign of consideration and empathy.

Emotional Well-Being: Healthy boundaries contribute to emotional well-being by preventing emotional overwhelm, burnout, and exhaustion.

Safety: They create a sense of safety and security, reducing the risk of emotional manipulation, coercion, and abuse.

Identity and Self-Expression: Boundaries allow individuals to express their unique identity, needs, and values without compromise.

Healthy Relationships: Well-defined boundaries are crucial for establishing and maintaining healthy relationships. They foster open communication, trust, and mutual respect.

Practical Strategies for Setting and Maintaining Personal Boundaries

Establishing and maintaining personal boundaries requires intentional effort and self-awareness. Here are practical strategies to help you define and maintain your boundaries:

Self-Reflection: Take time to reflect on your values, needs, and comfort zones. Understand what is important to you in various aspects of life.

Identify Boundaries: Determine what boundaries are necessary for your well-being in different areas, such as relationships, work, and personal space.

Communicate Clearly: Articulate your boundaries clearly and assertively to others. Use "I" statements to express your feelings and needs without blaming or accusing.

Practice Self-Care: Prioritize self-care activities that nurture your physical, emotional, and mental health. Self-care is an essential component of maintaining boundaries.

Learn to Say No: Saying "no" when necessary is a powerful boundary-setting skill. It's okay to decline requests or invitations that don't align with your boundaries.

Boundaries in Relationships: Establish boundaries in your relationships, including family, friends, and romantic partnerships. Communicate openly with loved ones about your needs and limits.

Recognize Manipulation: Be aware of manipulation tactics and emotional blackmail that can violate your boundaries. Stand firm against such behaviors.

Seek Support: If you struggle with setting or maintaining boundaries, seek support from a therapist or counselor. They can provide guidance and strategies.

The Role of Privacy in Setting Boundaries

Privacy plays a pivotal role in the establishment and preservation of personal boundaries. Here's how privacy and boundaries intersect:

Personal Space: Privacy allows individuals to define their personal space and decide who can enter it. It includes physical spaces like homes and bedrooms.

Emotional Privacy: Emotional privacy enables individuals to keep their thoughts, feelings, and experiences to themselves or selectively share them with trusted individuals.

Autonomy: Privacy safeguards individual autonomy and the right to make personal choices without external interference.

Safety: Privacy can create a sense of safety and security, especially in situations where personal information needs to be protected.

Respect: Respecting someone's privacy is a way of acknowledging their boundaries and showing respect for their autonomy and personal choices.

Challenges in Maintaining Privacy and Boundaries

While privacy and personal boundaries are vital, there can be challenges in maintaining them:

Social Pressure: Social norms and expectations may pressure individuals to share more than they are comfortable with, making it difficult to maintain boundaries.

Fear of Rejection: Some individuals fear that setting boundaries may lead to rejection or conflict in their relationships, making it challenging to assert their needs.

Guilt: Guilt can arise when individuals prioritize their own well-being and boundaries over the needs or expectations of others.

Lack of Awareness: Some people may not be fully aware of their own boundaries or the importance of privacy, making it challenging to establish and maintain them.

Balancing Boundaries in Different Contexts

Boundaries can vary in different contexts, and finding the right balance is crucial:

Professional Boundaries: In a work setting, boundaries may involve defining working hours, personal space, and the separation of personal and professional life.

Friendships: In friendships, boundaries might include respecting each other's need for personal time, privacy, and emotional support.

Romantic Relationships: In romantic relationships, boundaries may involve open communication, respect for personal space, and understanding each other's emotional needs.

Family: With family, boundaries can involve establishing autonomy as an adult, setting limits on invasive questions, and defining personal space.

Privacy and personal boundaries are foundational for healthy relationships and individual well-being. They serve as protective shields against emotional harm, manipulation, and the erosion of personal autonomy. By understanding the significance of privacy and boundaries, actively setting and communicating your limits, and respecting the boundaries of others, you can cultivate empowering relationships and foster emotional well-being in all aspects of your life. Remember that boundaries are not walls but fences, allowing for connection while maintaining individual integrity and self-respect.

The Ethical Use of Automatic Writing

Automatic writing is a fascinating and enigmatic practice that involves harnessing one's subconscious or spiritual connection to produce written content without conscious thought. While it can be a tool for self-exploration, creativity, and personal growth, it also comes with ethical considerations. This exploration delves into the ethical use of automatic writing, examining the potential benefits and risks and providing guidance on responsible practice.

Understanding Automatic Writing

Automatic writing, also known as spirit writing or trance writing, is a process where individuals allow their thoughts or words to flow onto paper or a digital medium without conscious thought or effort. The practice has been used for various purposes, including:

Spiritual Guidance: Some practitioners use automatic writing to connect with higher spiritual entities, seeking guidance, wisdom, or insights from the spiritual realm.

Creativity: Writers and artists use automatic writing as a means to tap into their creative subconscious, generating ideas, stories, or art.

Therapeutic Release: Automatic writing can serve as a form of catharsis, allowing individuals to release pent-up emotions, process trauma, or gain clarity about their feelings.

Self-Exploration: It is often employed as a tool for self-exploration and introspection, helping individuals uncover hidden thoughts, desires, or beliefs.

The Ethical Considerations of Automatic Writing

While automatic writing can be a valuable tool, it raises ethical considerations that practitioners should be mindful of:

Informed Consent: When using automatic writing to connect with others or spirits, it's essential to have their informed consent. Without consent, it may infringe on their privacy or personal boundaries.

Truth and Authenticity: Practitioners should be transparent about their intentions and whether the content generated through automatic writing is their own thoughts, creative expressions, or messages from spiritual sources. Misrepresenting the origin of the content can be ethically problematic.

Privacy and Confidentiality: Automatic writing may uncover deeply personal or sensitive information. Practitioners must respect the privacy and confidentiality of their own and others' revelations.

Emotional Well-Being: Practicing automatic writing for therapeutic purposes should be done with caution. Delving into traumatic experiences without proper support or guidance can lead to emotional distress. It's crucial to prioritize emotional well-being and seek professional help when needed.

Benefits of Ethical Automatic Writing

Embracing ethical principles in automatic writing can lead to various benefits:

Personal Growth: Ethical automatic writing can foster self-awareness, self-acceptance, and personal growth, helping individuals better understand themselves and their inner world.

Improved Relationships: Practicing automatic writing ethically can enhance communication skills, empathy, and understanding, leading to improved relationships with others.

Creative Expression: Ethical use of automatic writing can unlock creativity and inspire artistic endeavors, whether in writing, visual arts, or other creative pursuits.

Spiritual Connection: For those seeking spiritual guidance, ethical automatic writing can deepen their connection to spiritual realms while maintaining respect for spiritual entities and their messages.

Responsible Practice in Automatic Writing

To practice automatic writing ethically and responsibly, consider these guidelines:

Set Clear Intentions: Define your intentions for automatic writing, whether it's for creativity, self-exploration, or spiritual connection. Having a clear purpose helps maintain ethical boundaries.

Respect Informed Consent: If you intend to use automatic writing to communicate with others or spirits, seek their informed consent and be transparent about your intentions.

Privacy and Confidentiality: Treat the content generated through automatic writing with respect and confidentiality, especially when it pertains to sensitive or personal information.

Self-Care: Prioritize your emotional well-being and self-care. If you uncover distressing or traumatic content, seek professional support or guidance.

Honesty and Transparency: Be honest about the nature of the content produced through automatic writing. If it is creative or personal in origin, acknowledge it as such to avoid misrepresentation.

Boundaries: Establish clear boundaries for your automatic writing practice. Determine when and where you will engage in it and respect these boundaries.

Verification and Validation: If you receive information or guidance from automatic writing, consider verifying it through other means, especially if it has significant implications for your life.

Ethical Dilemmas: If you encounter ethical dilemmas or challenges while practicing automatic writing, seek guidance from trusted mentors, therapists, or spiritual advisors.

Risks and Caution in Automatic Writing

While automatic writing can offer profound benefits, it's essential to be cautious and aware of potential risks:

Deception: In some cases, content produced through automatic writing may not come from the claimed source. Be discerning and critically evaluate the information received.

Emotional Distress: Engaging in automatic writing without proper support or guidance can lead to emotional distress, especially when confronting traumatic or distressing content.

Dependency: Overreliance on automatic writing for decision-making or guidance can lead to dependency on external sources rather than developing one's inner wisdom.

Spiritual Vulnerability: When connecting with spiritual entities, individuals may encounter both benevolent and malevolent sources. It's crucial to practice discernment and protection.

Cultural Sensitivity: Be culturally sensitive when engaging in automatic writing that draws from or appropriates spiritual or cultural practices. Respect and acknowledge the cultural origins and significance of such practices.

Automatic writing is a powerful tool for self-exploration, creativity, and spiritual connection. When practiced ethically and responsibly, it can offer numerous benefits and insights. However, practitioners must remain vigilant about informed consent, privacy, transparency, and their emotional well-being. By embracing ethical principles in automatic writing, individuals can navigate its transformative potential while respecting their own boundaries and those of others. Ultimately, ethical automatic writing is a journey of responsible exploration and growth, offering a deeper understanding of the self and the world around us.

Respect for Others' Privacy

Respecting others' privacy is a fundamental aspect of human interaction and a cornerstone of healthy, respectful relationships. It involves recognizing and honoring the boundaries and personal space of individuals, whether in personal, professional, or digital contexts. In this exploration, we'll delve into the significance of respecting others' privacy, understand the key principles behind it, and explore practical strategies for fostering trust and building strong, respectful relationships.

Understanding the Significance of Privacy

Privacy, in its broadest sense, refers to the right and need for individuals to control their personal information, thoughts, feelings, and space. Respecting others' privacy is crucial for several reasons:

Autonomy: Respecting privacy acknowledges and respects an individual's autonomy—their ability to make choices about what they share and with whom.

Trust: Trust is built on the foundation of privacy. When individuals feel that their boundaries are respected, they are more likely to trust and open up in relationships.

Respect: Respecting privacy is a fundamental act of respect for an individual's wishes and personal space. It demonstrates consideration for their feelings and boundaries.

Safety: Privacy creates a sense of safety and security. It allows individuals to protect themselves from unwanted intrusion or harm.

Healthy Boundaries: Respecting privacy helps establish and maintain healthy boundaries in relationships, preventing emotional and psychological harm.

Principles of Respecting Others' Privacy

Respecting others' privacy is guided by several key principles:

Consent: Seek consent before accessing or sharing someone's personal information, whether it's in a conversation, online interaction, or a professional context.

Transparency: Be transparent about your intentions when collecting or using personal information. Individuals have the right to know why you need their information and how it will be used.

Purpose Limitation: Only collect and use personal information for the specific purpose for which it was shared or for a purpose that the individual has consented to.

Data Security: Safeguard personal information to prevent unauthorized access, sharing, or data breaches. Use secure methods to protect sensitive information.

Data Minimization: Collect and retain only the minimum amount of personal information necessary to achieve the intended purpose.

Respect for Boundaries: Respect the boundaries and personal space of others, both in physical and digital contexts. Avoid invasive or unwarranted intrusion.

Practical Strategies for Respecting Others' Privacy

To foster a culture of respecting others' privacy in your interactions and relationships, consider the following practical strategies:

Active Listening: Pay close attention to what others share with you in conversations. Respond empathetically and avoid prying into personal matters unless they voluntarily open up.

Ask for Permission: Before sharing someone's personal information or photos, ask for their permission. This applies to both offline and online situations.

Online Privacy Settings: When using social media or online platforms, respect the privacy settings and preferences of others. Avoid sharing or tagging them in posts without their consent.

Confidentiality Agreements: In professional settings, use confidentiality agreements when handling sensitive or private information. Ensure that colleagues understand and respect these agreements.

Consent in Relationships: In personal relationships, establish clear boundaries and seek consent in intimate matters. Respect your partner's comfort level and never pressure or coerce.

Teach Privacy to Children: Educate children about the importance of privacy and boundaries. Teach them how to respect others' privacy and recognize when their own privacy is being violated.

Secure Data Handling: If you handle personal information in a professional capacity, follow best practices for data security and privacy compliance. Be transparent with individuals about how their data will be used.

Respecting Digital Privacy

In today's digital age, respecting others' digital privacy is just as important as offline privacy. Here are some digital-specific considerations:

Cybersecurity: Protect your own and others' digital privacy by using strong, unique passwords, enabling two-factor authentication, and being cautious about sharing personal information online.

Social Media Etiquette: Be mindful of what you share on social media and the potential impact on others. Avoid sharing sensitive or private information about others without their consent.

Email and Communication: Respect the privacy of email and other digital communications. Don't share personal messages or information without permission.

Cookies and Tracking: Be transparent about the use of cookies and tracking on websites and seek user consent where required by privacy regulations.

Data Sharing: When using digital services or apps, review and adjust privacy settings to control the sharing of personal data. Understand how your data is being used by service providers.

Challenges and Common Pitfalls

Respecting others' privacy can face challenges and pitfalls:

Assumptions: Assuming that others have the same privacy preferences as you can lead to misunderstandings and boundary violations. Always seek explicit consent or clarification.

Invasive Curiosity: Avoid the temptation to pry into someone's personal life or to snoop on their personal information, whether online or offline.

Ignoring Boundaries: Ignoring or dismissing someone's expressed boundaries is a serious breach of privacy and trust. Always respect the boundaries set by others.

Failure to Correct Mistakes: If you accidentally breach someone's privacy, acknowledge the mistake, apologize, and take corrective action to prevent it from happening again.

Respecting others' privacy is a foundational aspect of building trust and maintaining healthy, respectful relationships. Whether in personal, professional, or digital contexts, it is essential to prioritize the autonomy, boundaries, and feelings of others. By following ethical principles and practical strategies for respecting privacy, we contribute to a culture of trust, empathy, and respect in our interactions with others, both online and offline. Remember that respecting privacy is not just a legal obligation; it is a fundamental expression of our regard for the dignity and autonomy of every individual.

Chapter 8
Advanced Techniques

This chapter explores advanced techniques in the practice of automatic writing, taking practitioners deeper into the art and science of this intriguing practice. It delves into methods for enhancing the quality and depth of automatic writing, offering insights into how to tap into higher levels of creativity, intuition, and self-discovery.

Automatic Writing with Tarot or Oracle Cards

Automatic writing, a practice that involves channeling thoughts and words without conscious effort, can be enhanced and deepened when combined with the use of Tarot or Oracle cards. This fusion of divination and creativity creates a unique synergy, unlocking profound insights and inspirations. In this exploration, we'll delve into the fascinating world of automatic writing with Tarot or Oracle cards, examining its benefits, techniques, and how to embark on this creative and intuitive journey.

Understanding Automatic Writing with Tarot or Oracle Cards

Automatic writing with Tarot or Oracle cards involves using these card decks as tools to trigger intuitive and creative responses in your writing. The process typically follows these steps:

Card Selection: Choose a Tarot or Oracle card or a spread of cards. These cards are often chosen intuitively or based on a specific question or intention.

Contemplation: Spend time contemplating the chosen card(s). Absorb the imagery, symbolism, and emotions they evoke. Let your mind and intuition engage with the cards.

Automatic Writing: Begin writing without conscious thought. Let the cards act as catalysts, guiding your writing in response to the insights, emotions, or ideas they trigger.

Flow and Intuition: Allow the writing to flow freely. Don't censor or judge your words. Trust your intuition and the guidance of the cards.

Benefits of Automatic Writing with Tarot or Oracle Cards

The fusion of automatic writing and Tarot or Oracle cards offers several benefits:

Enhanced Intuition: The cards can amplify your intuitive abilities, helping you access deeper insights and guidance.

Creative Inspiration: Automatic writing can stimulate creativity and innovation, making it a valuable tool for artists, writers, and creative thinkers.

Self-Discovery: This practice can lead to profound self-discovery and self-reflection, as it often unveils hidden thoughts, emotions, and desires.

Clarity: Tarot or Oracle cards can provide clarity on specific questions or challenges, helping you make informed decisions.

Spiritual Connection: For those on a spiritual journey, this practice can foster a deeper connection with higher guidance, inner wisdom, or the Divine.

Techniques for Automatic Writing with Tarot or Oracle Cards

To embark on the journey of automatic writing with Tarot or Oracle cards, consider these techniques:

Set an Intention: Before drawing cards, set a clear intention or question for your automatic writing session. This provides focus and direction to your exploration.

Card Spreads: Experiment with different card spreads, such as single-card draws, three-card spreads, or larger layouts. Each spread offers a unique perspective and depth.

Quiet Your Mind: Begin with a short meditation or mindfulness practice to calm your mind and connect with your intuition. This sets the stage for more focused and intuitive writing.

Journaling: Use a dedicated journal or digital document for your automatic writing sessions. The act of physically writing or typing can enhance the connection between your thoughts and the cards.

Free-Flow Writing: Start writing without censoring or overthinking your words. Allow the writing to flow naturally, even if it seems unrelated to the cards at first.

Card Analysis: After your writing session, analyze the chosen cards and the content you've written. Look for connections, symbols, or insights that may have emerged.

Reflect and Interpret: Reflect on the writing and its relevance to your intention or question. Interpret the symbols, metaphors, and themes that arise.

Practice Regularly: Consistency is key to honing your skills. Practice automatic writing with Tarot or Oracle cards regularly to strengthen your intuition and creativity.

Interpreting Card Symbols and Imagery

Interpreting the symbols and imagery of Tarot or Oracle cards is a crucial aspect of this practice. Here are some tips for effective interpretation:

Trust Your Intuition: Trust your initial impressions and intuitive responses to the cards. Your intuition often provides valuable insights.

Symbolism: Pay attention to the symbolism within the cards. Symbols can carry personal meanings and trigger specific thoughts or emotions.

Emotions: Note the emotions or feelings evoked by the cards. Your emotional response can guide your writing and reveal hidden aspects of your thoughts.

Colors: Consider the colors within the cards. Different colors can convey distinct emotions and messages.

Numerology: If you're using Tarot cards, explore the numerological significance of the cards. Each number has its own meaning and influence.

Recurring Themes: Observe if certain themes or symbols repeat in your card selections. Repetition can signify important messages or patterns in your life.

Context: Consider the context of your automatic writing session and your life circumstances. How do the cards relate to your current situation or question?

Maintaining Ethical Considerations

When practicing automatic writing with Tarot or Oracle cards, it's essential to maintain ethical considerations:

Consent: If you're exploring someone else's question or situation, ensure you have their informed consent. Respecting their privacy and boundaries is paramount.

Intention: Set clear and ethical intentions for your automatic writing sessions. Avoid using this practice to invade others' privacy or manipulate situations.

Confidentiality: Treat the content of your automatic writing sessions with respect and confidentiality. Don't share personal insights or information without permission.

Avoid Manipulation: Refrain from using this practice to manipulate or control others. Ethical use of automatic writing is about self-discovery, guidance, and creativity, not coercion.

Automatic writing with Tarot or Oracle cards is a dynamic fusion of intuition, creativity, and divination. It offers a profound opportunity for self-discovery, inspiration, and insight into life's mysteries. By incorporating ethical considerations and practicing regularly, you can embark on a transformative journey that deepens your connection with your inner wisdom and the guidance of the cards. Whether you seek personal growth, creative inspiration, or spiritual guidance, this practice can serve as a valuable tool on your journey of exploration and self-expression.

Channeling and Spiritual Guidance

Channeling is a mystical practice that involves connecting with higher spiritual entities or sources of wisdom to receive guidance, insights, and messages. This esoteric art has been pursued for centuries by individuals seeking a deeper understanding of the universe, their life purpose, and the mysteries of existence. In this exploration, we'll delve into the fascinating world of channeling and spiritual guidance, examining its history, techniques, and the potential benefits it offers to those who embark on this profound journey.

Understanding Channeling and Spiritual Guidance

Channeling is the process of allowing oneself to become a conduit or channel for spiritual or higher-dimensional energies, entities, or wisdom. Those who engage in channeling believe that it allows them to receive information, teachings, or messages that transcend ordinary human knowledge and experience. This practice typically involves the following elements:

Channel: The individual who facilitates the connection with higher spiritual entities is often referred to as the "channel" or "medium."

Spiritual Entities: These can include angels, ascended masters, spirit guides, extraterrestrial beings, or other non-physical entities believed to possess wisdom and insights beyond the human realm.

Communication: During a channeling session, the channel opens themselves to receive information, either through spoken or written words, automatic writing, or even non-verbal transmissions of energy and knowledge.

Purpose: Channeling is often pursued for various purposes, including gaining spiritual insights, receiving guidance on life decisions, healing, and personal growth.

Historical Perspective on Channeling

The practice of channeling has deep historical roots and can be traced back to ancient civilizations and spiritual traditions. Here are a few examples of channeling throughout history:

Oracle of Delphi: In ancient Greece, the Oracle of Delphi was a priestess who channeled the god Apollo's messages to seekers. Her trance-like state and cryptic responses were believed to convey divine wisdom.

Sufi Mysticism: Sufi mystics in Islam have a tradition of seeking divine guidance through altered states of consciousness, including trance and ecstatic dancing, to connect with the divine.

Spiritualism Movement: In the 19th century, the Spiritualism movement gained prominence, with mediums claiming to communicate with the spirits of the deceased. Séances and automatic writing were common practices.

New Age Movement: Channeling experienced a resurgence in the New Age movement of the 20th century. Various channelers claimed to connect with entities like Ramtha, Seth, and Abraham, offering spiritual teachings and guidance.

Techniques and Methods of Channeling

Channeling can take on various forms and methods, each with its unique approach and rituals. Here are some common techniques employed by practitioners:

Meditation: Many channelers begin with meditation to quiet the mind and raise their vibrational frequency, making it easier to connect with higher realms.

Automatic Writing: Some channelers use automatic writing, allowing a higher entity to guide their hand and write messages, often in a trance-like state.

Trance Channeling: Trance channelers enter a deep altered state of consciousness, often allowing a spiritual entity to speak through them in their own voice.

Sound and Chanting: Sound, such as chanting, drumming, or singing, can induce altered states conducive to channeling.

Crystals and Tools: Some channelers use crystals, pendulums, or other tools to enhance their connection and receive messages.

Guided Visualization: Guided visualization exercises can help channelers establish a mental bridge to higher realms, facilitating communication.

Benefits of Channeling and Spiritual Guidance

Channeling and receiving spiritual guidance can offer various benefits to individuals seeking deeper understanding, healing, and personal growth:

Spiritual Insights: Channeling can provide profound spiritual insights, helping individuals gain clarity about their life purpose, karmic lessons, and spiritual journey.

Guidance for Life Decisions: Seekers often turn to channelers for guidance on important life decisions, relationships, career choices, and health matters.

Healing and Emotional Release: Channeling can facilitate emotional healing by allowing individuals to release past traumas and unresolved emotions.

Connection with Higher Self: It fosters a deeper connection with one's higher self and spiritual essence, promoting self-awareness and self-realization.

Interactions with Spirit Guides: Channeling provides a means to communicate with spirit guides or guardian angels who can offer protection, guidance, and support.

Expanded Consciousness: It can expand one's consciousness and awareness, offering new perspectives on reality and the nature of existence.

Ethical Considerations in Channeling

As with any spiritual or mystical practice, channeling comes with ethical considerations:

Informed Consent: Channelers should obtain informed consent from individuals who seek their services. Seekers have the right to know and understand the process and its potential outcomes.

Integrity: Practitioners should maintain integrity by accurately representing the source of the messages or insights received during channeling sessions.

Confidentiality: Respect the privacy and confidentiality of those who share personal information or seek guidance.

Boundaries: Maintain clear boundaries between the channeling session and other aspects of life. Avoid exploiting or manipulating seekers for personal gain.

Critical Thinking: Encourage seekers to maintain a degree of critical thinking and discernment when interpreting messages received through channeling.

Channeling and spiritual guidance provide a fascinating avenue for exploring the mysteries of consciousness, spirituality, and the interconnectedness of all existence. Whether you approach it with curiosity, seeking guidance, or as a means of self-discovery, channeling can offer profound insights and transformative experiences. It is a practice that invites individuals to delve into the depths of their own consciousness and connect with the vast reservoir of wisdom believed to exist beyond the physical realm. As with any spiritual journey, approaching channeling with respect, ethical awareness, and discernment can lead to meaningful and enlightening experiences on the path of self-discovery and spiritual growth.

Collaborative Writing with Your Subconscious: Unleashing Creativity and Insight

Collaborative writing with your subconscious is a captivating and innovative approach to creative expression, self-discovery, and personal growth. It involves engaging with the deeper layers of your mind to access untapped creativity, insight, and inspiration. This exploration delves into the concept of collaborative writing with your subconscious, offering insights into what it is, its benefits, and practical techniques for unlocking its potential.

Understanding Collaborative Writing with Your Subconscious

Collaborative writing with your subconscious involves tapping into the vast reservoir of your unconscious mind to co-create written content. It is an imaginative process where you consciously engage with the deeper, often hidden, aspects of your psyche to produce creative work. Here's how it works:

Conscious Engagement: You consciously initiate the process by setting an intention to collaborate with your subconscious. This can be for various creative endeavors, such as writing poetry, stories, journaling, or exploring personal insights.

Relaxation and Mindfulness: To connect with your subconscious, it's essential to create a relaxed and receptive mental state. Techniques like meditation, mindfulness, or deep breathing can be helpful.

Automatic Writing: Begin writing without conscious thought or premeditation. Allow your thoughts and words to flow freely onto the page. The goal is to bypass the critical, analytical mind and access deeper layers of creativity and intuition.

Trust and Surrender: Trust the process and surrender to the flow of words. Avoid overthinking, editing, or censoring your writing during this phase.

Exploration and Interpretation: Once you've completed your writing, take time to explore and interpret the content. Look for themes, symbols, and insights that may have emerged from your subconscious.

Benefits of Collaborative Writing with Your Subconscious

Engaging in collaborative writing with your subconscious can yield a myriad of benefits:

Enhanced Creativity: By accessing the subconscious mind, you can tap into a wellspring of creativity and inspiration that often remains untapped in the conscious state.

Self-Discovery: This practice can lead to profound self-discovery, allowing you to uncover hidden beliefs, desires, and aspects of your identity.

Problem Solving: Collaborative writing can be a tool for problem-solving and generating innovative solutions to challenges in various areas of your life.

Stress Reduction: The act of writing in a relaxed, meditative state can be soothing and stress-reducing, promoting mental well-being.

Artistic Expression: Artists, writers, and creators can use collaborative writing to break through creative blocks and generate new ideas for their projects.

Personal Growth: As you explore the content generated by your subconscious, you may gain insights that contribute to personal growth, healing, and transformation.

Practical Techniques for Collaborative Writing with Your Subconscious

Here are practical techniques to facilitate collaborative writing with your subconscious:

Set Clear Intentions: Before you begin, set a clear intention for your collaborative writing session. What do you hope to achieve or explore? Having a specific focus enhances the process.

Choose a Relaxing Environment: Find a quiet and comfortable space where you can relax and write without distractions. Consider playing calming music or using aromatherapy to enhance relaxation.

Mindfulness Meditation: Start with a mindfulness meditation session to calm your mind and create a receptive state. Focus on your breath and let go of racing thoughts.

Automatic Writing Practice: Begin writing without conscious thought. Don't worry about grammar, punctuation, or coherence. Let the words flow naturally.

Stream of Consciousness: Embrace a stream-of-consciousness approach, where you write whatever comes to mind, even if it seems unrelated or nonsensical at first.

Time Limit: Set a specific time limit for your writing session. This can help you stay focused and prevent overthinking.

Reflect and Interpret: After your writing session, take a break and return to your writing with fresh eyes. Reflect on the content and interpret any themes, symbols, or insights that emerge.

Dialogue with Your Subconscious: Consider engaging in a written dialogue with your subconscious. Ask questions, seek guidance, and allow your subconscious to respond through writing.

Journaling: Use a dedicated journal or digital document for your collaborative writing sessions. Over time, you can track your progress and insights.

Consistency: Regular practice is key to deepening your connection with your subconscious. Set aside time for collaborative writing on a consistent basis.

Interpreting Subconscious Content

Interpreting the content generated through collaborative writing with your subconscious requires a blend of intuition and introspection. Here are some tips for effective interpretation:

Symbolism: Pay attention to symbols, metaphors, and recurring themes in your writing. These can carry deeper meaning and insights.

Emotional Resonance: Note the emotions and feelings that arise as you read your writing. Emotions often provide clues about the significance of the content.

Personal Relevance: Reflect on how the content relates to your current life circumstances, concerns, or aspirations. Your subconscious may be addressing specific aspects of your life.

Patterns and Trends: Over time, observe patterns and trends in your collaborative writing. Are there consistent messages or themes that emerge?

Open Dialogue: Maintain an open and ongoing dialogue with your subconscious through your writing. Ask follow-up questions and seek further clarification when needed.

Ethical Considerations and Boundaries

While collaborative writing with your subconscious is a personal and introspective practice, it's important to maintain ethical considerations:

Privacy: Respect the privacy of your own thoughts and emotions. Avoid sharing your collaborative writing with others without your consent.

Boundaries: Set clear boundaries for what you are willing to explore and share with your subconscious. Be mindful of your emotional well-being during the process.

Self-Care: Prioritize self-care and emotional support if you encounter challenging or distressing content during collaborative writing sessions.

Honesty: Approach the process with honesty and authenticity. Be willing to explore uncomfortable or hidden aspects of yourself with integrity.

Collaborative writing with your subconscious is a journey of self-discovery, creativity, and personal growth. By accessing the depths of your mind and engaging with your innermost thoughts and feelings, you can uncover profound insights, inspiration, and solutions to life's challenges. This practice invites you to explore the vast landscape of your consciousness, forging a unique partnership between your conscious and subconscious selves. With patience, consistency, and ethical mindfulness, collaborative writing with your subconscious can become a transformative tool for harnessing the power of your inner world to enhance your outer reality.

Conclusion

In conclusion, the practice of collaborative writing with your subconscious is a powerful tool for unlocking creativity, gaining insight, and fostering personal growth. By tapping into the depths of your mind and engaging in a creative dialogue with your subconscious, you can discover hidden talents, explore profound ideas, and find solutions to life's challenges. This practice invites you to embrace the vast potential of your inner world and offers a pathway to self-discovery and creative expression. With dedication and ethical mindfulness, collaborative writing with your subconscious can be a transformative journey that enriches both your creative endeavors and your understanding of yourself.

The Transformative Power of Automatic Writing

Automatic writing, a unique and transformative practice, has the power to unlock hidden depths of creativity, provide profound insights, and foster personal growth. By accessing the wellspring of your subconscious mind, automatic writing can be a catalyst for self-discovery and creative expression. This exploration delves into the practice of automatic writing, its historical roots, techniques, benefits, and its potential to transform your life.

Understanding Automatic Writing

Automatic writing is a form of written communication that emerges from the subconscious or unconscious mind without conscious thought or intention. It often involves a stream of words, ideas, or images flowing onto paper or a digital document as if directed by an unseen hand. Key elements of automatic writing include:

Subconscious Engagement: Automatic writing engages with the subconscious mind, bypassing the filters of the conscious mind to access deeper thoughts, emotions, and insights.

Intuitive Flow: During an automatic writing session, writers allow their intuition to guide them without premeditation or self-censorship. The goal is to let the writing flow freely and authentically.

Purposeful Exploration: Automatic writing can be employed for various purposes, including self-reflection, creative inspiration, problem-solving, and spiritual connection.

Historical Roots of Automatic Writing

Automatic writing has a rich history and has been practiced in various forms across cultures and time periods:

Spiritualism Movement: In the 19th century, automatic writing gained popularity during the Spiritualism movement. Mediums claimed to communicate with spirits of the deceased, channeling messages through automatic writing.

Surrealism: In the early 20th century, the Surrealist movement embraced automatic writing as a means of tapping into the unconscious mind to create art and literature.

Psychology: Carl Jung, a renowned psychologist, explored automatic writing as a tool for accessing the deeper layers of the psyche. He viewed it as a means of discovering the "collective unconscious."

New Age Movement: In the latter part of the 20th century, automatic writing saw a resurgence within the New Age and spiritual communities. Practitioners sought guidance from higher sources or their own inner wisdom.

Techniques for Automatic Writing

Embarking on an automatic writing journey requires certain techniques to establish a conducive environment and mindset:

Preparation: Find a quiet, comfortable space free from distractions. Set a clear intention for your writing session. This could be a question you want to explore or a goal you want to achieve.

Relaxation: Begin with relaxation techniques, such as deep breathing or mindfulness meditation, to calm the mind and reduce mental chatter.

Stream of Consciousness: Start writing without conscious thought or judgment. Let words flow naturally, even if they seem unrelated or nonsensical at first. Don't worry about grammar or punctuation.

Consistency: Practice automatic writing regularly to build a stronger connection with your subconscious mind and access deeper insights.

Reflection: After your writing session, take time to review and reflect on what you've written. Look for patterns, themes, and insights that may have emerged from your subconscious.

Benefits of Automatic Writing

The practice of automatic writing offers a wide range of benefits that can positively impact your life:

Creativity: Automatic writing is a powerful tool for stimulating creativity. It can help artists, writers, and creators break through creative blocks and generate innovative ideas.

Self-Discovery: Automatic writing often reveals hidden thoughts, emotions, and desires, leading to profound self-discovery and a deeper understanding of one's inner world.

Problem-Solving: The intuitive nature of automatic writing can aid in problem-solving and decision-making by providing fresh perspectives and solutions.

Stress Reduction: Engaging in automatic writing in a relaxed, meditative state can reduce stress and promote mental well-being.

Emotional Release: It offers a safe space for emotional release and catharsis, allowing individuals to process and let go of unresolved emotions.

Spiritual Connection: For those on a spiritual journey, automatic writing can facilitate a deeper connection with higher guidance, inner wisdom, or spiritual insights.

Common Misconceptions about Automatic Writing

Despite its many benefits, automatic writing is sometimes met with misconceptions and skepticism:

Uncontrollable or Supernatural: Some believe that automatic writing is uncontrollable or has supernatural origins. In reality, it is a controlled practice that taps into one's subconscious mind.

Only for Writers: Automatic writing is not exclusive to writers. Anyone can practice it to gain insights, stimulate creativity, or explore their inner world.

Lack of Conscious Control: While automatic writing involves bypassing conscious thought, it does not mean a loss of control. Writers can stop the process at any time.

Always Positive: Automatic writing can bring up both positive and challenging insights. It's important to approach the practice with openness and a willingness to explore all aspects of one's consciousness.

Automatic writing is a transformative practice that empowers individuals to tap into their inner wisdom, enhance their creativity, and embark on a journey of self-discovery. By creating a bridge between the conscious and subconscious minds, automatic writing unlocks the potential for profound insights, personal growth, and artistic expression. Whether you're seeking answers to life's questions, overcoming creative blocks, or simply exploring the depths of your own psyche, automatic writing can be a powerful tool for transformation and empowerment. Embrace it with an open heart and a curious mind, and you may find that its transformative power extends far beyond the page.

Encouragement and Final Thoughts

As we conclude our exploration of automatic writing and its transformative potential, I want to offer you encouragement and some final thoughts to empower you on your creative and introspective journey. Automatic writing is not just a practice; it's a pathway to self-discovery, creativity, and personal growth. By engaging with this process, you've embarked on a remarkable voyage into the depths of your consciousness. Here are some words of encouragement and reflection to carry with you as you continue your exploration:

Trust Your Intuition and Inner Wisdom

As you practice automatic writing, remember that you possess an innate wellspring of intuition and inner wisdom. Trust yourself and your inner guidance. Your subconscious mind holds valuable insights and creative potential waiting to be unearthed. Allow yourself to surrender to the flow of words and ideas, knowing that within you lies a well of creativity and wisdom.

Embrace Imperfection and Vulnerability

One of the most beautiful aspects of automatic writing is its capacity to reveal the raw, unfiltered essence of your thoughts and emotions. Embrace imperfection and vulnerability in your writing. It's okay if what emerges on the page doesn't always conform to conventional standards or expectations. In these unguarded moments, you often discover the most authentic and profound expressions of your inner world.

Persistence and Consistency Are Key

Like any skill or practice, automatic writing benefits from persistence and consistency. Make it a regular part of your routine. The more you engage with this process, the deeper your connection with your subconscious mind will become. Over time, you'll notice patterns, themes, and insights that emerge consistently, enriching your journey of self-discovery.

Embrace Self-Compassion

Be kind and compassionate toward yourself during your automatic writing sessions. If you encounter challenging emotions or thoughts, remember that this practice is a tool for healing and self-reflection. It's natural to uncover aspects of yourself that may be difficult to face, but through self-compassion, you can navigate these inner landscapes with grace and understanding.

Seek Inspiration from Within and Without

While automatic writing is a deeply introspective practice, don't hesitate to seek inspiration from external sources as well. Books, art, nature, and the wisdom of others can serve as catalysts for your own creativity and self-exploration. Draw upon the world around you to enrich your inner world.

Balance Self-Exploration with Action

Automatic writing can be a profound tool for self-exploration, but remember that its insights and creative sparks are meant to inspire action. Use the revelations and ideas that emerge from your writing as stepping stones to manifest positive changes in your life. Whether it's pursuing a creative project, making a decision, or embarking on a new path, let your automatic writing empower you to take meaningful action.

Connect with a Community

Sharing your experiences and insights with a community of like-minded individuals can be incredibly enriching. Seek out or create a space where you can connect with others who share an interest in automatic writing. Engaging in discussions, sharing your writings, and hearing about others' experiences can provide valuable support and inspiration.

Revisit and Reflect

Periodically revisit your previous automatic writing sessions. Reflect on how your insights and understanding have evolved over time. You'll likely notice growth, changes in perspective, and a deepening connection with your subconscious self. These reflections can be a source of motivation and encouragement.

Final Thoughts

In the world of automatic writing, there are no limits to the depths you can explore or the heights you can reach. This practice invites you to embark on a journey of self-discovery that has the potential to transform your life, your creativity, and your relationship with your own mind. It's a tool for embracing the full spectrum of your consciousness—the light and the shadow, the known and the mysterious.

Remember that the power of automatic writing lies within you, and it's always available to you, ready to unveil new layers of your inner world. Approach each session with an open heart and a sense of wonder, and you'll find that the blank page is a canvas for the colors of your soul.

Your journey with automatic writing is a unique and personal one. It's a journey of self-exploration, creativity, and empowerment. It's a journey that can lead to profound insights, healing, and the discovery of your true self. Embrace it with enthusiasm and curiosity, and know that every word you write brings you closer to the transformative potential within you.

As you continue to engage with automatic writing, may you find the courage to embrace your authenticity, the wisdom to navigate the depths of your subconscious, and the inspiration to live a life that aligns with your deepest desires and aspirations. Your journey is a testament to the power of self-discovery and creative expression, and it is an ongoing source of growth, transformation, and fulfillment.

www.ingramcontent.com/pod-product-compliance
Lightning Source LLC
LaVergne TN
LVHW061528070526
838199LV00009B/418